The
Heinous Murders
of 21st Century Women

The Hitmen Were Wearing Judge's Robes

The Heinous Murders of 21st Century Women

The Hitmen Were Wearing Judge's Robes

By Shirley J Foor

INTERROBANG

Bradenton, Florida

Library of Congress Cataloging in Publications Data
ISBN 979-8-9891662-2-0

Published by Shirley J Foor
Interrobang, Bradenton, Florida
First edition

Editor: Sharon E. Fay
Book Design by Nancy Koucky

This is a work of nonfiction.
Opinions expressed here are those of the author.

Dedication

The words herein and the passion with which they
were written are dedicated to every woman
and every family terrorized and damaged by the
arrogant, ignorant lawmakers who have made
deadly medical decisions
without benefit of medical training or license.

Pithy and Pertinent

Every time we turn our heads the other way
when we see the law flouted,
When we tolerate what we know to be wrong,
When we close our eyes and ears to the corrupt
because we are too busy or too frightened,
When we fail to speak up and speak out,
We strike a blow against
freedom, decency, and justice.

— Robert F. Kennedy

Table of Contents

Author
Shirley J Foor

Shirley Foor began as a freelance writer when she was a young stay-at-home mom. When her husband broke his back, she became the breadwinner for her family of six. Shirley was hired as a features writer at *The Daily Dispatch*, a local daily newspaper in Illinois. As her skills improved, she advanced to a beat reporter, to bureau chief, and to assistant editor of the regional department. She was declared unqualified and denied a promotion to regional editor but received a timely invitation to interview for the city editor's position at *The Bradenton Herald* in Florida. She moved her family to Florida to become the first female city editor and then the first female managing editor at *The Herald*.

After 20 years in journalism, Shirley retired. She continues to write and to regularly publish creative nonfiction stories for a subscriber list of family and friends.. In addition to writing, Shirley also is a photographer. She began as a photo-journalist to improve her strength as a journalist. She also has published three creative-nonfiction books of common daily experiences that touch us all, and her first major work, *It's Okay to be Gay—God How man rewrote Scripture to justify his bigotry. The Heinous Murders of 21st Century Women* is her second major nonfiction work and is based upon her years of journalistic practices.

Introduction

Once upon a time, when the world was new and God still retained a reverential hold on humanity, woman was revered. God gave her major responsibilities, which have been well recorded throughout the Old Testament. Female prophets. A female judge named in Scripture. A female priestess. Female church leaders.

Women enjoyed positions of authority and decision-making and teaching. Women leaders were part of the Biblical landscape. God selected them for their skills and their talents, not because no male was available to do the job.

You see, God created two humans, a man and a woman. By his careful words in Genesis, He established woman as man's equal. "Then God said, 'Let us make human beings in our image, in our likeness. They will reign over the fish in the sea and the birds in the sky, the livestock and all the wild animals and all the creatures that move along the ground.'" Genesis 1: 26-27 NIV.)

They will reign, he said. To reinforce His intention, He named both humans Adam, another word for humankind. (Genesis 5:2)

Then, with the fall of the Adam's family in the Garden of Eden, God began to lose control of His balanced plan for the continued and orderly Creation of mankind.

Adam blamed the female Adam for his lack of integrity and leadership. And God. Oh, yes, he did. The male Adam blamed God for giving him the woman who offered him the forbidden fruit. Adam accepted no responsibility for anything.

In time, the Jews blamed the woman for Adam's lack of character. She not only was responsible for Adam's fall in the Garden of Eden, but she also must not be trusted. She had, after all, led the male Adam to sin.

Woman shall not speak to or teach man about God. Woman must submit to her husband. Woman's dishonor intensified throughout history, until man rendered her irrelevant in her servitude to him.

The once implicit patriarchy has grown impudent in its ignominious intent to betray God's trust in Team Mankind. Century by century, man has perverted God's plan with the careful-but-faulty pruning of Scripture. Scripture by Scripture, man has meticulously selected snippets of Scripture to persuade woman that God had indeed granted him supremacy by proxy.

Alas, none of the patriarchy's prohibitions, under which women have lived for eons, came as directives from God. Instead, they are man's careful extractions from the Gospels. The black-letter words contain the recollections of Jesus' teachings and work, as recorded by scribes. The red-letter text are the words of Jesus. If the Scripture is not in red letters, then it is man's recollections.

When Christ died on the cross, he fulfilled the laws of the Old Testament. An eye-for-an-eye became do unto others as you would have them do unto you. Love your neighbor as you love yourself. The Old Testament and its esoteric litany of laws and taboos about various and sundry concerns became a history lesson.

In death, Christ died for our sins and granted us a clean slate and a full measure of grace every day. If we repent of our sins, we begin anew each day.

In death, Christ brought us the New Testament, which embraces love, equality, and free will. Man, ever the opportunist, has run afoul of the gift of free will in his pursuit of his fraudulent authority over women.

As I said earlier, God planned that each Adam would play

different and distinct role in the tasks He had set before them. Regardless of their differences in abilities and attitudes, the individuals were, nonetheless, created to work as a team. Kind of like the majestic Clydesdale horses in a hitch. Two strong individuals, side by side, holding joint dominion over all the world. God had faith in His humans.

Given the turn of history, I think it is possible that as man has diminished the female half of God's Team Equality, he also vexes God's spirit. God had granted woman an equal role. However, man has seized upon the smallest points in Scripture to discredit woman's place next to him.

For instance, God's scribes used the Greek word *ezer* to describe the female Adam's role in Creation. According to scholars of the Greek language, the word in this context means, "a partner equal to the male Adam." Responding to his ego, man selected a lesser meaning of *ezer*. He chose "helpmate," which in his mind and in practice reduces woman to his servant, not the person who works as his equal. Eventually, the patriarchy decided that man fully owns the woman.

For centuries, the unbalanced hitch has continued to pull toward the male Adam's side. And, for centuries, the hitch has been traveling in circles, like the Israelites circled Mount Seir in discontent on their journey to the Promised Land. Deuteronomy 33:2.

The result of the persistent pull in the male Adam's direction? The birth of a pernicious patriarchal leech that presumes to suck out a woman's life blood.

Since at least the early 1800s, when the male-dominated law-making bodies introduced abortion laws, man has controlled woman's prerogatives.

During that time, history shows that woman was considered "breeding stock," so to speak, which man controlled with his abortion laws. He was compelled to ensure that the "right kind" of babies were produced to protect the white patriarchy. White women of that time were having a baby only every two years or so. Women of color were producing babies much more often. The patriarchy focused on saving every white child, most particularly the white male babies.

The white slave owners of the day conveniently overlooked their acts of rape and impregnation of their slave women. On the other hand, they held white women to account for their sexual activity by preventing abortions that might eliminate a white male child.

Everything a woman was belonged to the patriarchy. A woman's thoughts and her personal decisions. Even to her health-care and to whom she listens for her important health-care advice.

Current-day lawmakers affirm that the patriarchy, and the patriarchy alone will determine if a woman has the right to live and how she will live as a breeder.

Full disclosure: I write this nonfiction narratives with an attitude. I am purely worn out from talking around and around the truth, thereby excusing man's total cock-up of his macho decision-making.

Man, who was created with one set of attributes, was to partner with woman, who was created with attributes that complement his. God's Creation intent exists only in man's rearview mirror. His male attributes of strength, courage, fierceness, absent the stability of the female attributes of care, caution, nurturing, and attention to detail, among others, have led to waring, whoring, pedophilia, and human trafficking, among other travesties of male power.

Since the 18th century, the male-dominated state legislatures have added the blatant and willful killing of woman by ill-conceived laws in the name of the patriarchy. Women will carry every baby to term, no matter what.

As a woman of more than 70 years' experience working in a man' world, 50 of those years to support my disabled husband and five children, I am outraged. I am even more outraged that man has manipulated the hounds of justice to chase the fox of abortion.

Hear my outrage! The real target in preserving the rights of women to life and liberty lies in hounding out of existence the wolves, the male-dominated state legislatures that rabidly enact one *unconstitutional* abortion law after another.

For 20 of the years in which I supported my family, I was a print journalist when journalism was wholly a man's world. I received assignments the male reporters didn't want to handle, was paid $2 less an hour than even the new male reporters, and endured the snide remarks because I was the Queen of Crappy Assignments. Me supporting my family also was less important than a man supporting his.

During those 20 years I learned to ask question after question in search of the truth when the "facts" didn't add up to a logical explanation. Or when the "fact" just didn't "smell right." The overturning of Roe v. Wade dredged a fetid malodorous swamp of smells and many questions.

While I am fully engaged in calling out men who are so full of themselves that they have no compunction in killing and maiming women to protect the white patriarchy, I do not consider all men rude, crude, and obnoxious dolts.

I respect and pay homage to the countless exceptional men who stand tall for the inventions that have enhanced our lives. The men who have discovered life-saving drugs and procedures that help us to live longer and better. Still others who have created magnificent art. And then there are the countless men who contribute to their communities. I have known and revered many in my various hometowns.

To woman's misfortune, though, we must deal daily with the aforementioned men. The ones who power their way through women's lives, destroying instead of creating for the good of mankind and following God's plan.

We need a fuller understanding of the dwindling and fearful patriarchy. We need a better understanding because this powerful group employs Scripture to manipulate and to ensure that we trust their word. Sadly, our unerring trust in their words, their patriarchal interpretations of God's word, has sabotaged our very existence.

For instance, the insistent voices that repeat man's many scriptural misinterpretations have deadened woman's ability to think and to question. We trust implicitly; we fail to question explicitly.

For every Scripture with which man celebrates his contrived dominance, a nearby Scripture has a "think again" contradiction. However, man has conveniently overlooked those ironies. For example, 1 Corinthians 7:4 (AMP) says, "The wife does not have [exclusive] authority over her own body, but the husband *shares with her;* …" The men stick to those words like flies stick to flypaper.. But, wait! There's more. The part of the Scripture that men skip over. "… and likewise, the husband does not have [exclusive} authority over his body, but the *wife shares with him.*" How old were you when learned about that Scripture?

Man's cavalier use of sacred Scripture to inflate his position betrays his allegiance to God's words of Creation. Consequently, man has systematically eliminated that annoying *equality* stuff, to enslave women. Since the advent of the New Testament and free will, man has made it his hallowed mission to limit woman's equality in *his* domain.

Before you get your knickers in a knot, I do not believe that *all* women are so trusting or so gullible. Nor do I believe that *all* men think they have the right to decide a woman's fate. *All* is God's realm, not mine. It is clear, however, that we women are in this abortion mess because enough of both genders agree with the current practice of the patriarchy suppressing women's rights writ large.

Over the centuries, man's power over and determination to control women has gained breath-taking strength. Roused by the gift of free will, man has been free to choose his path, any path, and to walk it in his self-determined way. In that freedom and in his quest for scriptures that prove he is the master of woman, he has become king of scriptural cherry pickers. His phony Biblical pronouncements also are a constant pain in a woman's soul and a perpetual threat to her life.

The astounding spread of man's pernicious patriarchy was

exacerbated by Donald J. Trump, the 45th president of the United States, for whom strong women are a threat. He pledged that he, as president, would end a big threat: a woman's rights under Roe v. Wade.

So, with some behind-the-scenes skullduggery, Trump packed the Supreme Court. He appointed three double-speak judges to become Supreme Court justices. To ensure that the antiabortion allies would be confirmed, Trump directed certain government agencies to suppress documents and in-person testimony against the antiabortion nominees.

In June of 2022, Supreme Court of the United States accomplished the joint goal of Trump and Justice Samuel Alito: kill Roe v. Wade.

To my female reader, I say that we women have been and continue to be hustled. God did not abandon His plan for woman's integral participation in dominion over all. Neither did He nor Jesus ever condemn abortion. Nor did He anoint man with the authority to kill and to maim women.

God and His son, Jesus, valued women throughout the history of His word. On the other hand, as has been evinced in the years since Roe v. Wade was overturned, man has become vindictive in his power over women. His intent is clear. Woman's worth lies in preserving the white patriarchy.

In recent actions, those esteemed lawmakers have imposed court-sanctioned and state-legislated genocide of women. Invigorated by the encouragement of the powerful in federal government, the state lawmakers continue to refine their laws to be broader and more barbaric and deadly. They know nothing of the tribulations of pregnancy, the dangers of giving birth, or the medial reasons that may require an abortion. Nor do they invest any time in learning. They answer only to their ego needs.

To put it plainly, the abortion bans began two hundred years ago for the very purpose of making sure that more of the right color of babies were born than the "other" kind.

So that you have a better understanding of how man has manipulated women's circumstances to affect our demise as individuals, we begin *The Heinous Murders of 21st Century Women* with woman's current crisis of trust and threat to her life and liberty.

Through the chapters, we'll work our way from the obscene and dishonest decisions of the Senate Judiciary Committees that put three deceitful SCOTUS justices on the high Court.

We shall examine, too, the abhorrent majority decision to overturn Roe v. Wade and raise some serious questions about whether the Supreme Court had the authority to independently overturn Roe v. Wade.

Additionally, we shall lay at the feet of the patriarchy their full responsibility for all—*all*—unwanted pregnancies. The very pregnancies for which they hold women responsible and punish them. We women have let men play at our expense—our physical, mental, emotional, and financial expense.

In their unbridled freedom, man has created countless unwanted pregnancies. We women have failed to exercise and to stand firm in our rights as human beings.

In the name of transparency, much of my research herein is based upon the work of male scholars who have escaped the influence of the male-only echo chamber of scriptural misinterpretation.

It is time for a woman's point of view of our God-granted equality. It is time for a woman's point of view on the despicable Supreme Court decision that has assured state-granted and unconstitutional genocide of females across our nation.

By their detestable actions, the male-dominate legislatures have declared, repeatedly, that we women are not worth the price of our participation in humanity.

As my research will show, man has reduced woman's place in history to the equivalence of "breeding stock," in the name of assuring the white supremacy and its patriarchy.

The malevolence behind the scenes—the misinterpretation of the Bible, the Red Cult of the Supreme Court justices and the Red

Cult legislatures rejection of constitutional law—that has permitted the genocide and the mutilation of the patriarch's breeding stock is the motivation for this book.

We begin my challenging narrative with a timely review of history, Biblical and recent, and woman's place in it. The story opens with the tale of Sodom (Genesis 19; 1-28) in a 20th century setting.

Modern-Day Sodom Visits the Senate

The story of Sodom (Genesis 19:5-13) is one of depravity and destruction.

God sent two angels, disguised as men, to the city of Sodom. Lot, a new resident in Sodom, saw two strangers while he was sitting in the gateway to the city. It would have been dangerous for the strangers to be out alone at night, so Lot invited them to the safety of his home.

They had barely finished dinner when a mob of men—both young and old—from every part of the city surrounded the house.

"Where are the men who came to you tonight? Bring them out so that we can have sex with them." Different versions of the Bible vary from "have sex with them," to "know them," to "know them carnally," to "know them intimately." Regardless of how the Bible's scribes worded the demand, we know for darn sure that the men were not there for vigorous game of dominos.

Lot went to the door and protested. "No, my friends. Don't do this wicked thing. Look, I have two daughters who have never been with a man. Let me send them out to you, and you can do what you want with them. But don't do anything to these men who have come under the protection of my roof."[7]

Hearing Lot's words, the mob raged still more. Lot, too, was a newcomer to the city, and the men loudly objected to the stranger telling them what to do.

Well, the angels hastily pulled Lot back into the house and saved the daughters from certain death by keeping them inside. They told Lot to round up everyone who meant anything to him and get out of town. [12]"Do you have anyone else here—sons-in-law, sons or daughters, or anyone else in the city who belongs to you? Get them out of here, [13]because we are going to destroy this place. The outcry to the LORD against its people is so great that He has sent us to destroy it." By "this place," the angels meant all of Sodom.

Flash forward to September 27, 2018.

The scene opens on the Senate Judiciary Committee in the Rayburn House Office Building in Washington, D.C. This prestigious committee is engaged in questioning Judge Brett Kavanaugh, the newest nominee to be a Justice on the Supreme Court of the United States (SCOTUS). His coveted nomination has been momentarily threatened by a woman.

In this version of Sodom, Sen. Lindsay Graham plays the role of Lot. Kavanaugh is the guest in Lot's house, the Senate committee room. The crowd comprises the woman, Christine Blasey Ford[1], who has accused Kavanaugh of raping her at a party when she was 15, and those witnesses who want to be heard on the Ford's behalf. However, the crowd is not menacing or demanding. It stands at the ready in the wings, watching the hearing on television.

The woman, who has been sworn in, is seated at the witness table. During the committee's questioning, the derision toward the female was palpable. The male senators were insolent and menacing. If anyone within earshot of the publicly televised proceeding thought the woman, a respected research psychologist at Palo Alto Univesity in Northern California, would receive a fair and productive hearing, then that person also believes in leprechauns and pots of gold at the ends of rainbows.

A member of the committee asked that the Federal Bureau of Investigation (FBI) properly examine the allegation against

Kavanaugh. Again, the appearance of leprechauns was a greater possibility than an honest investigation.

You see, the Red Cult of Personality, Trump's loyal minions, was hard at work behind the scenes. The Red Cult reflected the intentions of the Red Cult Master (RCM), Donald J. Trump, the 45th President of the United States, a man of amoral and immoral character.

Trump wanted Kavanaugh confirmed to the federal bench. He believed this man would vote to overturn Roe v. Wade. He was correct.

For 50 years, this law had ensured woman's protection for specialized health care, specifically abortion. In his confirmation hearing, Kavanaugh had testified that Casey v. Planned Parenthood, which backed up Roe v. Wade, had settled the matter. The law was settled precedent, he said. Kavanaugh especially satisfied the prominent female members of the Red Cult, who had bought into his silver-tongued testimony and his personal assertions, made in their Senate offices.

During the hearing, Lot Graham snarled at Kavanaugh's accuser, baring his teeth and contorting his face in anger, like a growling animal. He raged about how no one, especially someone like her and her supporters, had the right to accuse this outstanding jurist. He praised Kavanaugh, "who comes to the bench with the finest of qualifications." Graham, the Senator from South Carolina, said that he would not "be a participant in the wholesale character assassination" that defies credibility. (More on the "flawless" Kavanaugh in a later chapter.)

Lot Graham totally disrespected the woman who came to the hearing with a credible concern about Kavanaugh's honesty and integrity. Lot Graham's performance was stunning, and he authoritatively slammed the door against the outside threat.

In truth, Lot Graham was, and still is, a principal in the District of Columbia branch of moral eunuchs who bow and scrap before the Red Cult Master. Graham's actions assured Kavanaugh's successful confirmation.

For Kavanaugh's part, he, too, ranted and snarled. He performed as an aggrieved smart-ass frat brat in front of Senator Amy Klobuchar. He insulted her and treated her as an underling. He cried and raised his voice, and he snarled again, indignant in his "distress." The committee chairman did not admonish the nominee for disrespecting the female Senator.

Professor Jennifer Oliva of West Virginia University College of Law, one of 900 law professors objecting to Kavanaugh's appointment, commented on Kavanaugh's behavior. "Turning the questions back on Senator Klobuchar was an outrageous act," she noted. "Such disrespectful antics cannot be erased with an after-the-fact apology. Instead, it reflected a real problem with dealing appropriately with women in positions of power."[2]

Kavanaugh refused to answer questions from the committee, especially the questions from the Democrats, the non-cult members. Kavanaugh had no need to answer questions from them. He knew he was in the clear. The chairman of the Judiciary Committee, Sen. Chuck Grassley, had suppressed hundreds of pages of information regarding Judge Kavanaugh's questionable history. (More on this in Chapter 4)

From my perspective, Graham's and Kavanaugh's performances were little more than contrived, amateurish, and embarrassing to the official proceeding. Nonetheless, both performances were allowed to stand as though nothing untoward had happened in the respected chamber.

Kavanaugh's outrageous behavior also aroused the ire of 2,400 law professors[3] in more than 190 law schools. In reproach, the professors sent a letter to the Judiciary committee. "Judges must step aside if they are at risk of being perceived as or of being unfair ... We have differing views about the other qualifications of Judge Kavanaugh," they wrote. "But we are united, as professors of law and scholars of judicial institutions, in believing that Judge Kavanaugh did not display the impartiality and judicial temperament requisite to sit on the highest court of our land."[3]

Their considered viewpoints carried no weight whatsoever with the esteemed Senate Judiciary Committee. Trump had spoken, and the moral eunuchs feared his wrath.

Even the female Red Cult senators fell in line. They dismissed Ford's assertions about Kavanaugh and ignored the many people who awaited their opportunity to speak on her behalf.

Another letter came to the committee. This one was from 800 female law school faculty asking the Senate to reject Kavanaugh's appointment. "All of us believe that Judge Kavanaugh's partisan performance and unprofessional behavior during his testimony on September 27 disqualify him for the most important judicial position in our country," explained Professor Kathleen Engel of the Suffolk University Law School[4].

In a separate email, Karla McKanders, a professor of law at Vanderbilt University Law School, said, "As a law professor, it is my responsibility to teach my students the highest standards of professionalism and decorum. Judge Kavanaugh's testimony undermines the legal profession and would undermine the authority of the Supreme Court."[5]

The moral eunuchs in the Red Cult-dominated Senate Judiciary committee cared not at all about the opinions of these knowledgeable persons. Impervious to the overwhelming professional opposition to Kavanaugh's confirmation, the committee continued to talk about Kavanaugh's "integrity" as a jurist.

In fealty to Trump, the Red Cult delivered the prize: Another important vote on the Court that he needed to assure the overturning of Roe v. Wade.

So, in the best Sodom fashion, Lot Graham saved the man, Kavanaugh, from the truth of the crowd's objections and the calls for his accountability. The woman turned into a pillar of salt, or at least into the subject of further derision, after her abusive spurning.

The "investigation" did not include testimony from any of the men and women ready to testify on behalf of Ford. From the wings, the Red Cult Master declared that the investigation, such as it was, found the man to be squeaky clean. Kavanaugh was confirmed to the lifetime position on the supreme court. The vote? The Red Cult, 50; the Party for Truth, Justice, and the American Way, 48.

Before I continue, we need to talk about the Red Cult of Personality. This cult controls all thought within one political party in our two-party system. The Washington, D.C. branch of the cult and those among the states take their cues from the RCM, whose personality reeks of amorality and immorality.

In case you are unfamiliar with the word cult, as most of us are, a cult of personality is the misplaced or excessive admiration for a particular person or thing. People in cults lose their sense of individuality and their ability to think or to act for themselves, become obsessed with cult doctrine, and frequently end contact with loved ones in deference to the cult's rule.

The result of the Red Cult Master's nominations and the confirmations of Kavanaugh and other justices will be exposed as we compare the overturning of Roe v. Wade to Judges 19-21. One hasn't lived until one encounters the abomination that is Gibeah in Judges. Our visit to Gibeah replicates the Red Cult's arrogant disdain for woman as a group. The cult certainly does not see women as equal partners as God declared. Satan eagerly feeds the craven cult's insatiable need for power and aggrandizement.

Sodom and Gomorrah, and symbolically the Judiciary committee's chamber, are now smoking embers. Lot protected the man in his house to the detriment of the woman. Lot Graham and other committee members sacrificed Ford and withheld information pertinent to Kavanaugh's confirmation and laid waste to the once honorable deliberations in the committee room.

Our visit to Gibeah also will replicate how the powerful Red Cult senators and SCOTUS betrayed their oaths to uphold the Constitution and have cruelly subjugated women to the service of the white patriarchy.

Justice Alito Brings Gibeah
to the 21st Century

The story of Sodom was a Mother Goose tale compared with what happened in Gibeah. The story of the rape of the concubine and its aftermath, as written in Judges 19:22-30, is darker than the darkest of tales from the brothers Grimm.

If you do not know the story of Gibeah, read it now, for the first time.

A Levite was traveling from Bethlehem with his concubine. They got as far as Gibeah when night began to fall. An old man, returning from the hill country of Ephraim, saw the man and woman in the city square. He wondered if they had accommodations for the night. Being out in the open was a dangerous proposition.

As was the custom of the time, the old man, who lived in Gibeah, brought the Levite and his concubine home to stay. Although the Levite assured the man that he had all he needed to camp out, so to speak, he wisely accepted the man's hospitality.

As they settled in for the night, some thugs from the city pounded on the old man's door, demanding that he [22] "Bring out the man who came to your house so we can have sex with him. The thugs, all Benjamites, wanted to rape the man. Rape was how men asserted their dominance in the patriarchy. Still is.

Well, the old man, being the considerate and protective host that he was, offered an alternative. It is best that you read the words from Judges 19: 23-30 to gain the full weight of the old man's perverse plan. [23] The owner of the house went outside and said to them, "No, my friends, don't be so vile. Since this man is my guest, don't do this outrageous thing. [24] Look, here is my virgin daughter, and his concubine. I will bring them out to you now, and you can use them and do to them whatever you wish. But as for this man, don't do this outrageous thing."

Women were wholly irrelevant to men, so the two men sacrificed their women to protect the Levite. Nothing more was mentioned of the daughter, but the concubine became the gift that kept on giving unto death.

The next day, the Levite threw the woman's lifeless body onto the back of his donkey. The gang-rape death of his concubine was nothing of consequence. He had been complicit in the old man's generosity and protection and had submitted his woman to the brutality that killed her. Wasn't his problem, though.

When the Levite arrived home, in his best chest-beating style, he was indecently angry at the Benjamites who had raped his concubine. To show his anger, he [29] "... took a knife and cut his concubine, limb by limb, into twelve parts and sent one piece to each region of Israel's inheritance, because they [the Benjamites] committed this lewd and outrageous act in Israel.

[30] "Everyone who saw it was saying to one another, 'Such a thing has never been seen or done, not since the day the Israelites came out of Egypt. Just imagine! We must do something! So, speak up!'"

Please note here that the Levite presented himself not only as devoid of blame but also without a conscience. For instance, he said the men in Gibeah had come to kill him. He couldn't admit that the men had demanded to have sex him, which would make him look weak. (Note from the author: today's man insists that the men in Judges were participating in homosexual acts. Not so. The intent of the mob was to engage in brutal sodomy, outright male-to-male rape.)

The Levite also couldn't say that he had sent his woman (and she was *his* woman) into the street to be raped while he and the old man cowered in the house. He cared nothing for his concubine in life or in death. Upon his return home, he casually dismembered her. In spite, the Levite sent his concubine's bloody body parts to each of the twelve the tribes of Israel to incite them to battle against the tribe of Benjamin.

Well, the Levite was successful. A major battle ensued between the Benjamites of Gibeah and the Israelites.

Of course, the battle was necessary. Men had violated the Levite's property, his woman. The Benjamites had killed his woman in the land of Israel, so, naturally, the Israelites must arm themselves and fight the Levite's battle to avenge the loss of his property and to restore his honor.

The Levite remained safe while hundreds of thousands of Benjamites and Israelites died to avenge the loss of his property in the conflict he had perpetrated.

Fast forward to June 22, 2022, and the Supreme Court's specious decision to abandon protected abortion care for women by over-turning of Roe v. Wade.

In one petulant, self-serving act, Justice Samuel Alito became the Levite of all time. He dismembered the body of womanhood writ large and sent the pieces into all the lands governed by the Red Cult legislatures. There, goaded by the false prophets of the vengeful religious cults, the moral eunuchs in the Red Cult legislatures eagerly inflicted more torment in the name of "saving a *potential* life."

Vexed by what he believed was an "egregious decision,"

handed down 50 years earlier, Levite Alito had waited decades for the "right" justices to assemble, vindicate his opinion, and overturn the Roe v. Wade precedent. At last! The band of sympathetic justices had been delivered to the bench

I call this assembly a "covert unit." The future nominees to the antiabortion unit had carefully led their confirmation committees to believe that the 50-year-old decision was safe with them.

The nominees had cloaked their "belief" that Roe v. Wade was precedent in politic padding. Kavanaugh was the exception. In his testimony, under oath, he said Roe. V. Wade and Casey v. Planned Parenthood had underscored the strength of the law. "… one of the most important things to keep in mind about Roe v. Wade is that it has been reaffirmed many times over the past 45 years, as you know, and most importantly, most importantly, reaffirmed in Planned Parenthood v. Casey in 1992."[6]

He said the words and implied support; However, he didn't say he would uphold the intent of those words.

Important to this part of the narrative is the fact that each nominee was seeking his appointment to the coveted lifetime position on the revered SCOTUS bench. Caution was imperative. Speaking truthfully about this touchy issue could jeopardize their confirmation to the sacred judicial bench.

Now that he had the full complement of abortion eunuchs in place, Levite Alito, a peevish and richly entitled old man, made an even more egregious decision. The decision that unleashed an unholy war against any woman able to bear a child.

Not only did Alito remove the protection of the constitutional precedent, but in his entitlement of power he also said the several states should, once again, be granted the right to decide a woman's personal health choices.

In my research, some important questions surfaced.

- The official case before the Court was Dobbs v. Jackson Women's Health Organization. The health organization was asking the Court to review the constitutionality of Mississippi's law banning abortion after 15 weeks of pregnancy. The Court upheld the Mississippi law. How did Roe fit into this specific case?

- The overturning of Roe v. Wade did not appear as an official case before the Court. No writ of certiorari had been presented for judicial review, as provide by Court procedures. If there were no contesting entities, who had standing to bring the case to revoke the long-standing law? What Court process permitted the Court to independently overturn constitutional law?

- Did Alito have the authority, the standing, to instigate the revocation of established precedent and overcome the doctrine of stare decisis?

- Alito said the Constitution contained no language about abortion. So, if the federal document bears no words for or against the abortion, how does a woman's decisions about her health care belong to the Court and the states, but not to her?

- Did Alito, in his position of entitlement, tacitly approve of a state legislature's breach of a woman's Constitutional rights?

Alito's egregious and disdainful transfer of power from a woman, granted in Section 1 of the Fourteenth Amendment, to the elected officials in the states that have no authority under the Constitution rankled my sense of justice.

Levite Alito's decision made it clear that, to him, woman is as insignificant as the ant he stepped on as he walked toward the stately building that houses the Supreme Court building. He was committed to righting the "egregious decision" the SCOTUS from 1972 to satisfy his thesis and his bloated ego. Throughout the majority opinion, Alito falsely focused on what the states wanted and the rights to which, he insisted, the states and the elected representatives were entitled.The majority's disdain for the rights of women is recorded in brazen emphasis. Throughout the opinion, the focus was on what the states wanted, the rights to which the states and the elected representatives were entitled. Those states had banned abortion from the beginning, and they wanted their rights back.

I must say that my outrage over Alito's willful, waspish overturning of this monumental precedent makes it impossible to respect him with the honorific of *Justice*. Justice was not even a consideration for him. For a man in this significant position of authority, his entitlement of great judicial power and trust, to impose his opinion so callously, makes him the insignificant ant under my footfall.

Actually, now that I think about it, that's exactly how I feel about the majority voice on the Court. Self-serving, self-important, and slavish to the Red Cult Master. Acutely unworthy of the trust placed in their hands. And the evidence of their deceit and entitlement mounts.

Today, in many states, because of the unconscionable willfulness of the Supreme moral eunuchs, women can be jailed for a miscarriage, a God created spontaneous abortion, unless the woman can prove its legitimacy. By what right do these barbarians hold a woman to account for an act of God?

On behalf of women, I say, I believe Levite Alito had no authority to overturn Roe. v. Wade. No writ of certiorari from a lower court was offered; no one on the Court had standing to introduce an independent proposition. Determination and vindictiveness was driving the bus of judicial righteousness to Revocation.

Full disclosure, I did seek some legal opinions on my thinking. The opinions affirmed my theory that, among other considerations, the Court lacked standing. Then, I wrote to two constitutional specialists, who shall remain nameless in their disrespect and their apparent complicity. I explained that I was including the Court's decision in a book and posed the questions and premise that I have presented within this narrative. As of publication, neither authority favored me with even the most cursory acknowledgment of my request for clarification.

So, hearing no objections to my view of the facts, I have proceeded in the belief that I am correct in my conclusions. I believe the constitutional gurus would have corrected a wrong premise.

To my way of thinking, the business of a woman's decision to have an abortion is *no business* of any state. The Supremacy Clause, the Ninth Amendment and the Fourteenth Amendment confirm my beliefs. Now, women are being terrorized by what, in my view, are unconstitutional laws imposed by the moral eunuchs in the Red Cult. Yes, I believe these abortion bans are illegal. (More on this in another chapter.)

Equal protection under law seems to be a moveable feast of jurisprudence when it comes to women's rights. Thanks to Alito's peevishness, women living in the states with Red Cult legislatures no longer have the same protections as women living in other states. They have become defenseless prey before the wolves in Red Cult jurisdictions.

Roe v. Wade had granted women that equal protection. The Red Cult Supremes callously removed woman's equal protection under the color of law.

Based upon his words in the Roe v. Wade decision, Levite Alito gave little to no thought that his petulant act breached the "equal protection" code.

No one wants to question man's authority. Even if that authority is wrongly assumed. I believe, too, that this is why I heard nothing from the constitutional scholars. They don't hesitate to pontificate about the law in a detached manner. They relish their authority. Above all, though, they are not going to comment on how a man may have erroneously executed that law.

In the meantime, women across the country have been so busy trying to protect their lives, they can hardly think about what's next, or what remedies against the long-term abuse might be theirs.

In writing the majority decision, Levite Alito allegedly provided words for why he thought the 50-year-old decision was an egregious error. Applying the standard that I used when I tutored college freshmen in their writing assignments, his reasoning had a fog factor of 10 and failed to support his premise. He did not prove any "egregious action," only his petty grievance and his twisted thoughts and ancient, seemingly irrelevant law to support his thinking.

He provided incorrect information and unsupported assertions. He reached back to ancient law instead of considering the words of Chief Justice Charles Evans Hughes on judicial review. "This power of 'judicial review' has given the Court a crucial responsibility in assuring individual rights, as well as in maintaining a 'living Constitution' whose broad provisions are continually applied go complicated new situations."[7] Not a chance. Alito's actions were all about assuaging his grievance and serving the Red Cult Master.

The text of his life-changing decision is available online. Ironically, the decision is entitled *Dobbs v. Jackson Women's Health Organization*.[8] However, it is primarily about the overturning of Roe v. Wade.

After I had digested his word-salad justification for his action, I realized that not only did he not present a cogent, accurate argument for his thinking, but he also didn't have to be convincing. Oh, yes, he had a legal obligation to write the decision of the majority, but, in a phrase, "the fix was in." The majority of the once-respected robe wearers, befouled though those robes are from their current corrupt behaviors, are stuffed with Red Cult loyalists.

Whatever man declares is lawful at any given moment determines the extent of a woman's rights. He feels no compunction in his malevolent behavior toward women and the sanctity of women's constitutional rights. The woman in the Court's five-member cult majority joined into the decision because that was her role. The Federalist Society had promoted her to the RCM who fast tracked her nomination to the bench. Her thinking and record favored his, and she would be a good girl and play well with the boys on the bench.

To reiterate in explaining the court's decision, Alito said that the U.S. Constitution makes no reference to abortion rights. True enough. The Constitution is silent on the topic, and all other topics for that matter. No reference for or against the abortion.

Currently, consideration for the woman's health draws a distant second to the fervent, frenzied protection for a zygote, an embryo, a fetus, any stage of gestation. They ignore the Biblical certainty stated in Genesis 2:7 that life begins with the first breath, i.e., when the fetus emerges from the birth canal, takes its first breath, and cries out. The Red Cult covets the "promise" of a life more than it reveres the actual life of the woman who is carrying the promise.

Alito, in writing the majority decision, says: "We hold that Roe and Casey must be overruled. The Constitution makes no reference to abortion, and no such right is implicitly protected by any constitutional provision, including the one on which the defenders of Roe and Casey now chiefly rely—the Due Process Clause of the Fourteenth Amendment."[9] Let that sink in, Dear Reader. Alito believes that the Fourteenth Amendment does not apply to women's rights.

Let me propose a spoonful of thought that contradicts Alito's proclamations.

First, neither the Constitution nor the two amendments say anything about abortion. Because that is the case, then, logically, a woman may choose to do anything for her body and her continued good health. No permission is necessary from any government authority. The Ninth Amendment upholds that thought.

Second, both the Supremacy Clause of the Constitution

and the Fourteenth Amendment *restrict* the rights of states to the *upholding* of the Constitution. According to those superior documents, the states *may not* restrict rights, even the right to an abortion. However, each state may expand or protect rights, as many states and commonwealths and states are doing and have done.

Third, the states that are legislating potential genocide in the name of protecting a developing life are indeed violating a woman's right to life, liberty, and due process, in concert with Alito's permissive language.

The Supreme Court's decision to overturn Roe v. Wade was an atrocity too far for this octogenarian. Four men and one woman, with a thimbleful of humanity and conscience among them, promoted state-sponsored genocide. They call it "protecting the fetus." I call it giving license to ill-informed, knee-jerk legislators to make medical decisions that are well beyond the scope of their legal jurisdiction and their medical expertise.

Furthermore, it seems quite patronizing to suggest, much less believe, that a state has greater interest in protecting the fetus than the woman who is literally pouring her life into every step of gestation. How bumptious!

Basically, I believe the Red Cult legislatures are practicing medicine without the requisite license. Furthermore, a woman's private decisions are none of their business. To enact a law legalizing genocide of pregnant women who need or want abortions is a barbaric and cruel overreach of man's lawful authority. Neither the law nor God has granted man such absolute power.

No exceptions for rape or incest. No exceptions for children raped by a trusted adult. No right for any adult woman to decide with her doctor how to proceed with a serious health-care concern. No exception for an ectopic pregnancy. A cruelly forced pregnancy in every situation. All, I believe, are unconstitutional restrictions.

Also, please note, the Red Cult legislatures are full-throated in their condemnation of any woman who seeks to protect her health. However, these moral eunuchs remain silent when it comes to any corresponding mandate for a man to keep his pants zipped when he is not with his wife. That's an admonition in the Bible that's equal to "thou shall not kill," which man says the anti-abortion obsession is all about. Keep the non-descript fetus alive while killing or maiming the woman carrying the nonentity. Explain that deadly contradiction, please.

No. I am not a lawyer. But, my reader friend, I am at least as smart as the men who should know better about their obligations to the Constitution and to those who elected them to their entitled office. Furthermore, these elected officials took an oath of office to uphold the Constitution. Guess that fact escaped their minds in their orgasmic power surge.

Who am I to be outraged? I am the mother of five children who also had three spontaneous abortions, which God brought about, not I. Basically, I had no control over any of it. Though all eight pregnancies were unplanned, they were accepted. Four of my pregnancies were uneventful, and I was a healthy woman. The fifth birth nearly took my life. My pregnancies were unplanned because no woman controls or can predict her window of fertility. I could speculate, based upon the fallacious information passed down, woman to woman, but a pregnancy occurred by the coincidence of sperm meeting egg. On the other hand, the man is perpetually fertile and bears full responsibility for unwanted pregnancies. (More on this in Chapter 5)

Not unsurprisingly, the moral eunuchs, in their power surges, do not acknowledge that a man had even participated in creating every one of those pregnancies. Of course not. The man takes his pleasure and walks away. No penalties or obligations need be imposed. Virgin births, one and all.

A later chapter will establish how we women have allowed men to be irresponsible for their part in all—*all*—unwanted pregnancies. The practice of acceptable irresponsibility started, from my point of view, with their mommas' grossly indulgent, nauseating excuse that, "Well, boys will be boys, you know. They won't listen." In later years, women will excuse their husband's irresponsibility and disrespect with their sophomoric, mitigating, "Well, you know, men will be men."

Nonsense! With the incessant repetition of those mitigating platitudes, we have empowered men to be irresponsible Tom cats, at our expense. Currently, the Tom cats are aided and abetted by the moral eunuchs in the Supreme Court and in the Red Cult legislatures.

Once upon a time, the Supreme Court was revered. Someone seated on that bench was special. In my grade-school civics class, we learned about the awesome responsibility of the Court. That was in the days before the Red Cult of Personality oozed its way onto the Court.

Now, my heart hurts for the three distinguished female justices currently on the bench. They continue to fight for the law, even as the law is being crushed under the thumb of the Red Cult. Justice Steven Breyer, the eminent and well-respected justice who with justices Elena Kagan and Sonia Sotomayor, wrote the heartfelt dissenting opinion in the overturning of Roe v. Wade, also deserves appreciation. After the decision, Breyer retired from the bench.

Hopefully, the words in this chapter and throughout my nonfiction narrative will help women to understand that we must rethink our allegiance to man's right to remain irresponsible to our detriment and to control any part of our lives. Men have failed, egregiously, in their allegiance to the Constitution and to protect the lives of the women who helped elect them to office of entitlement. And women, who, like their own mothers, are the founts of all life.

God created woman as man's equal (Genesis 1: 26-27) Man has systematically diverted our attention from God's equality to subjugation under man's authority. In severing womanhood from the Constitution, the Red Cult majority Court nakedly continues man's imagined authority over women. The Roe v. Wade majority opinion provides painfully significant evidence of that fact.

Still more evidence of how easily man dismisses woman is found in the confirmation hearings of the Supreme Court nominees.

More on the heinous influence of the Red Cult of Personality coming up.

The "Fix" Was In

We have endured the Supreme Court's spiteful decision. Spiteful because no entity of any description had officially sought sought the overturning of the constitutional law. Furthermore, the majority of residents of every state support the continuation of abortion rights. Only the Red Cult, led by the 45th president of the United States, wanted abortion in the hands of legislators to control women and their baby-making rights. The repugnant, selfish, and deadly decision has yet to be fully suffered.

Nothing ever is as it seems on the surface. We know, for instance, that dozens of antiabortion laws have been enacted throughout the states since Roe v. Wade was overturned. We believe that those laws should be deemed unconstitutional because they violate a woman's constitutional right to life, liberty, and due process. Those laws also impose restrictions on a woman's healthcare that are not delineated in the U.S. Constitution or in the Bill of Rights.

Furthermore, we know that under the Supremacy Clause of the U.S. Constitution and the Fourteenth Amendment the state constitutions may be more expansive than the federal document, but not more restrictive. The antiabortion laws are not only restrictive, but they also take away a woman's right to protect her own life.

I have learned two important points in my research for this

book. For the first, the authority of the Bible is invoked when it suits man's purposes. When the authority of God's word works at cross purposes to man's intention, then, obviously, we have misinterpreted Scripture. For the second, quoting the Constitution is important, until it isn't. Just as the Bible provides a convenient authority to keep control of women, so does the Constitution. Man rejects either, or both, as he needs.

Based upon my observations of our world situation, the revocation of Roe v. Wade, man is more interested in stirring up trouble than he is in how to make our lives better.

Since the beginning of time and the moment God granted women equality in His plan for creation, men have arrogantly turned a blind eye to any law that does not fit with their air of entitlement.

I write to say that man's control over a woman's thoughts, a woman's choices, a woman's actions has existed for so long we no longer understand that we are being controlled. This is not a criticism of man, but an observation of how we women no longer remember, if we ever really knew and understood, that God created woman as man's equal. We certainly have not heard that fact from any pulpit.

I write to say that we women are in this predicament because the male-dominated Senate Judiciary Committees, so intent upon striping a women's constitutional right to make her own health choices, connived its way to success in packing SCOTUS with justices who are clones of the corrupt 45th president: gold-plated con artists, one and all.

I write to tell how two respected professional women tried to give evidence that two nominees for SCOTUS justices, Clarence Thomas and Brett Kavanaugh, were not the best examples of men who would uphold the law. We watched as Anita Hill and Christine Blasey Ford were demeaned, disrespected, and ridiculed by the male senators who would confirm those unfit men to the Court. However, Blasey Ford was not the only woman to cast aspersions on Kavanaugh's suitability for the bench.

This narrative is a look behind the scenes of how we gained

this eminently corrupt majority of jurists, under cover of the Red Cult of Personality. The information I share with you is readily available to anyone. Reliable web sites (government sites about the Constitution and the Supreme Court). Inexpensive, well researched books. Nothing mystical or magical will rise from my keyboard. These are simply facts that the reliable media lack the time, the will, and the news space and time to reiterate. The Red Cult of Personality has worked its devilish magic to deny women the respect, the justice, the privacy, and the due process promised in the Ninth and the Fourteenth amendments to the United States Constitution.

And to be very forthright in this narrative, I make no apology for my clear disdain for the majority voice on the Supreme Court of the United States. Respect is earned, and the overwhelming arrogance and corruption in the Red Cult majority on the Court cancels any respect I may have had.

Moreover, I write about these abhorrent manipulations of important information by government agencies and stewards of the Constitution because we have received only what the judiciary committees wanted us to know. Their surreptitious withholding of information and dishonesty in their actions have rendered women ignorant of and subject to enormous injustices.

We begin with the two justices—Clarence Thomas and Brett Kavanaugh—who seem to have an issue with women and the laws pertaining to their treatment of them.

In Chapter One, we reviewed how the men circled the wagons around Judge Kavanaugh during his SCOTUS confirmation hearing when a woman testified that he had raped her at a party when she was 15. The Senate Judiciary Committee made short work of the woman's reliability and respectability. They demeaned and embarrassed her with their crass theatrical performances.

An investigation into the allegation was ordered. Ordered, yes, but seriously truncated at the direction of the leader of the Red Cult of Personality, the 45th president of this once proud democratic republic. He shut down any legitimate pursuit of truth because Kavanaugh was an essential part of his plan to overturn Roe v. Wade.

However, Kavanaugh came with other baggage that tainted his fitness for office. Significant information was withheld and suppressed in many ways and by many people. I'll hit the high spots in the grand cover-up by the judiciary committee to give you a framework for the questions about Kavanaugh's baggage that never surfaced.

For instance, American Oversight, a nonpartisan, nonprofit watchdog "that advances truth, accountability, and democracy by enforcing the public's right to government records,"[10] filed at least four lawsuits to gain records pertinent to Kavanaugh's fitness for office. The records pertained to Kavanaugh's handling of possibly stolen documents and his questionable interactions with the Office of Legal Counsel during his time as legal counsel for President George W. Bush's administration.

American Oversight filed one lawsuit on behalf of six members of the Senate Judiciary Committee who sought records pertaining to Brett Kavanaugh's time as councilor to President George W. Bush. "The administration and Committee Chairman Chuck Grassley blocked access to records they deemed essential to fulfill their constitutional advice and consent responsibility."[11] All four cases resulted in government agencies withholding documents pertinent to requests from other groups seeking to more about questionable situations involving Kavanaugh.

Some of those records were withheld from the judiciary committee, again, by direction of President Trump. Others were withheld by the chairman of the Senate Judiciary Committee, Sen. Chuck Grassley. Still others were withheld or delayed in their release by the National Archives and Records Administration (NARA), and the Department of Justice (DOJ).[12]

This resource makes interesting reading about who was protecting the Nation's interests and who was bowing to the Red Cult Master.

Not surprisingly, the documents were not released in time for Kavanaugh's confirmation, and his suspect sleaziness was kept hidden from the confirmation committee. It's no wonder that Christine Blasey Ford experienced the reprehensible and disgusting behavior from the snarling Sen. Lindsay Graham, the sophomoric crying scene of Judge Kavanaugh, and other shameful displays. They didn't want her accusations to disturb the coverup to pack the Supreme Court with antiabortion sympathizers.

In the weeks prior to Kavanaugh's confirmation hearing, the Senate Judiciary Committee conducted three spontaneous telephone interviews with the candidate. None of them under oath. The committee already knew about Christine Blasey Ford's[13] planned testimony. Two other women, Deborah Ramirez[14] and Julie Swetnick[15], had brought complaints of Kavanaugh's sexual misconduct to the Senate Judiciary Committee. The committee decided to give Kavanaugh a sneak peek at the questions before his official confirmation hearing

The Senate Judiciary Committee questioned Kavanaugh three times by telephone, and not under oath or with his accuser present for the questioning. The interviews are billed as background, and they were transcribed.

The Democrats on the judiciary committee objected to the committee's favorable treatment of Kavanaugh and refused to participate. The names of the committee Republican members, all public servants, were redacted in the transcripts of these background sessions. According to the transcript of the Ramirez case, only one unnamed woman was present for Kavanaugh's defense of the accusations against him.

Curiously, in the Swetnick transcript, only one woman, the only Democrat ever present, was named. The transcriptions named Diane Feinstein, ranking member of the committee; the men's names were redacted.

As with Ford's complaint, an FBI investigation into the complaints was mentioned, but the information from these conversations with Kavanaugh were not entered into the record or submitted for further investigation. The chairman of the Judiciary committee, Sen. Chuck Grassly, dismissed the investigation into the accusations of Blasey Ford, saying that it would show nothing.

The nature of Kavanaugh's alleged actions and what the women allegedly were asked to do are too disgusting for me to include. The full committee did not hear the complaints of the two women, nor did it hear Kavanaugh's glib denials. The new complainants were silenced by their forced absence.

Clarence Thomas's confirmation hearing was another study in blatant gender discrimination. Anita Hill, a graduate of Yale law school, and Thomas, also a graduate of Yale law, worked in the U.S. Department of Education's Office for Civil Rights. Thomas was an assistant secretary, and Hill was his legal advisor. This is the timeframe in which Hill contended that Thomas engaged in sexual harassment.

During his confirmation hearing, the committee reluctantly pursued Hill's accusation against Thomas. She testified that Thomas "talked about pornographic materials depicting individuals with large penises and large breasts, involved in various sex acts ... On several occasions, Thomas told me graphically of his own sexual prowess."[16]

The committee chairman, Sen. Joe Biden, ordered the Federal Bureau of Investigation to investigate the allegations. Then, returning to the business of the hearing, the chairman said, "I believe there are certain things that are not at issue at all ... And that is his (Thomas's) character ... This (hearing) is about what he believes."[17]

Nina Totenberg, long-time Supreme Court reporter for National Public Radio, added to her report, "Speaking in warning tones, Biden added, 'I know my colleagues, and I urge everyone else to refrain from personalizing this battle.'"[18]

As a woman, I was immediately offended by the chairman's directive. Hill's testimony made abundantly clear that Thomas's character was very much involved. If he lacked accountability for his disgusting and abusive remarks to a female superior, how could he be counted on to render impartial decisions on the bench? It would seem to me that a jurist short on character and integrity should not be seated on the bench of the highest court in our land.

Thomas's current allegations of accepting questionable "gifts" from men with business before the federal Court very clearly demonstrates the importance of "character" to a member of the Court. Basic integrity also seems to elude Thomas's body of ethics, as it does other men on the Court.

During the hearing, Thomas's character and honor were protected; Hill's was not. She not only was disrespected but also maliciously castigated. Chairman Joe Biden failed to call for decorum on Hill's behalf. One senator accused Hill of "flat-out perjury." Another said her testimony was the "product of fantasy." Yet another said he thought she, "Got the idea for some of the charges from the movie *The Exorcist*."[19]

Still others asked, "Are you a scorned woman?" … "Are you a zealoting (sic) civil rights believer?" … "Do you have a martyr complex?"[20]

The men were not admonished to treat the witness with respect. By all means, protect the character of the accused male and belittle the character of the female accuser.

We women gullibly believe that because we help elect these men, these senators, to their esteemed office that they work for our interests, too. I believe the experiences of Anita Hill and Christine Blasey Ford attest to the contrary. The men on the respected judiciary committees did not trouble themselves to show respect to well-educated, well-respected women. Nor did the chairman admonish the members for their behavior.

The Judiciary Committee voted 13-1 to send Thomas's nomination to the full Senate. However, the nomination was forwarded without recommendation, which means that not everyone approved of his nomination.

As a woman, I feel confident that you, the reader, also could describe many incidents in which a lying male was given credence, and you were disparaged. I submit that this has become so commonplace that we no longer trouble ourselves to question it. We then fail to stand up for our integrity, our value, and our equality.

As with respect, equality is not given until we claim it. We have some work ahead of us.

Based upon news reports, we now know that Thomas and Alito are short on integrity. They have accepted money and favors from wealthy men with business before the Court. We also have learned that in addition to voting to overturn Roe v. Wade, Neil Gorsuch also has benefited from a real-estate transaction with a man whose law firm has frequently came before the Court.

The lack of character among these esteemed men of the law lay in their failure to disclose these lavish gifts. By virtue of their entitlement on the Court, they righteously impose rules upon others. However, they cavalierly spurn the rules of common decency, integrity, and transparency that apply to them. Their hypocrisy is abhorrent.

Our final moral eunuch is Amy Coney Barrett who displaced Thomas as the "least qualified" jurist to gain a seat on the high Court. (Thomas had a little more than a year on U.S. Court of Appeals for the District of Columbia.) In fairness, Barrett didn't seek the job of Justice. The Federalist Society, of which she is a member, recommended her to Trump, who imposed his will upon the judiciary committee. Basically, she was a suitable shill for the Red Cult.

Her experience comprises being a law professor at Notre Dame and three years as a federal appeals court judge. However, her lack of judicial experience was not so important as the assurance that she would play well with the boys and overturn Roe v. Wade. Which she helped to do.

As with Kavanaugh, Barret's appointment was questioned by outside agencies. For one, the New York City Bar Association questioned Barrett's fitness for the high Court. Its research on her history and her answers to her views on matters of law concerned the body greatly. The City Bar wrote that "... Judge Barrett lacks the temperament ... to search for a fair resolution of each case." As an example, City Bar wrote, "Judge Barrett's rejection of accepted science (climate change) on the grounds that it was controversial also raises concerns that she is not independent from the Executive Branch that nominated her and held and aggressively advocated the same views."[20]

The City Bar also called her out on her scholarly writings, which "suggest an eagerness to overrule long settled and revered Supreme Court precedents guaranteeing individual rights," such as Roe v. Wade, among others.

The City Bar provided numerous examples of Coney Barrett's inclination to eliminate precedent wherever and whenever possible. No matter. The Red Cult Master got what he wanted, and Samuel Alito was assured of his Red Cult majority.

We have touched upon Alito's questionable overturning of Roe v. Wade, but there is way more to examine in some detail. We women have simply taken for granted the states legislatures' authority to restrict our freedoms and to wantonly endanger our lives.

Did Alito have the authority to bring the question of Roe v. Wade before the Court? He had no standing or clearly described authority. Do the states have the constitutional right to restrict a woman's rights to life, liberty and due process of law as granted in the Ninth and Fourteenth amendments just because Alito decreed the entitlement to be so?

Details coming up.

Screwed by the Supreme Court

As a woman of sound mind, the body not so much, I have diligently tried to make sense of the SCOTUS decision to overturn Roe v. Wade.

The more I researched, the more outraged I became.

For the record, this book began as a nonfiction narrative about how God created woman as man's equal in their dominion over the world, and how man has successfully contrived to make her subservient. Man's actions, recorded in the Roe v. Wade obscenity, have redirected my pursuit of truth. Over the centuries, man has skillfully manipulated Scripture to attest to his assumed divine power over woman, a power that God did not intend.

The SCOTUS decision was the most abhorrent demonstration of man's blatant disregard for woman as an equal being, even as a human being for that matter. So complete is our enslavement that women are being consigned to death, destruction of reproductive organs, and forced pregnancies to "protect potential life," as Justice Alito wrote in the majority decision.

My outrage grew as the initiator of the appalling Court action, Justice Samuel Alito, got all huffy in a public interview because the public was being so unkind to the Court. The Court was just "doing its job," he said. My premise here and throughout *The Heinous Murders* is that the legislatures and the courts in the Red Cult states are breaking constitutional law to make unconstitutional law.

My outrage takes me well beyond where the women who are fighting for life-saving abortion rights. In my outrage, I am asserting that SCOTUS has disregarded the prescribed procedure for bringing questions of law for judicial review and, thereby, committed judicial rape-by-proxy of womanhood writ large. At the very least, the Court, quite simply, screwed woman because it could. Alito had his heart set on it.

To satisfy my questions and to quell my outrage, I drew upon my 20 years' experience as a journalist and asked question after question. The answers to those questions left me speechless.

For clarification, I have used a variety of sources, including government documents, for answers. All sources are readily available online. No secret code words or handshakes are necessary for you to learn what I have learned.

For the record, if you believe that I have misconstrued factual information, show me my error in an official document. Show me my error in specific words. If I have erred, I shall stand rightly scolded and correct my error. However, I do not want your "interpretation" of words that "appear" to support your theory of the information. I want to see the black words, printed in a reputable, dependable source that directly contradicts my research..

As I said in an earlier chapter, it defies logic that a single justice would have the power to initiate the overturning of 50 years of precedent. Powerful men routinely interpret text to suit their needs. Be that as it may, an act so important as overturning established law needs an explanation. There is one, and it is significant.

Let's start with my questions. The answers will help you to understand how the Court bamboozled us and misrepresented women in its decision.

What is the Court's role?

Basically, the Supreme Court has four roles. First, as the highest court in the land, it is the court of last resort for those seeking justice. Second, through its power of judicial review, it assures that the government recognizes the limits on its own power. Third, it protects civil rights and liberties by striking down laws that violate the Constitution. Fourth, it ensures that popular majorities cannot pass laws that harm and/or take undue advantage of unpopular minorities.[21]

Let's think about the fourth point for a minute. Popular majorities cannot harm unpopular minorities. Hmm. Do you see the irony here? The popular majority cannot harm the unpopular minority. However, the unpopular minority, six justices on the nine-member corrupt and out-of-favor Supreme Court, can summarily revoke a 50-year-old constitutional precedent favored by the popular majority of, say, 80% of the adults among our 332 million population. So much for the court looking out for "We, the people …" and our civil rights.

How does a case come before the Court?

To bring a regular case before the Court, the dissatisfied party in a lawsuit must file a writ of certiorari, asking the Supreme Court to review a lower court's decision. If the Court takes the case, the Court begins its judicial review.

Judicial review, instituted in 1803, *gives* the Court the "right to examine the actions of the legislative, executive, and administrative arms of the government and to determine whether such actions are consistent with the constitution."[22]

In addition, to maintaining a certain protocol, *The Court and Constitutional Interpretation*, written by Chief Justice Charles Evans Hughes (1930-1941), gives a more powerful view of the process. "This power of 'judicial review' has given the Court a crucial responsibility in assuring individual rights, as well as in maintaining a 'Living Constitution' whose broad provisions are continually applied to complicated new situations." Justice Hughes called attention to two significant points in judicial review: "… a crucial responsibility in assuring individual rights" and "… maintaining a 'Living Constitution.'"[23]

From my perspective, Alito and the majority missed the "assuring *individual* rights" and the "… maintaining a 'Living Constitution'" parts of the review process.

How is constitutional law changed?

Constitutional laws may be overturned in two ways. By bringing a new case from a lower court to the Supreme Court for judicial review or by amendment to the Constitution. For clarity "new" means "not existing before," or "of recent origin." These dictionary definitions are important for later in this narrative.

How did the Court overturn Roe v. Wade?

By judicial sleight of hand. Or maybe just little misdirection in the name of judicial authority.

The Court used Dobbs v. Jackson Women's Health Organization (Mississippi)[24] to covertly slide Roe v. Wade into the discussion. The deadly scam went something like this:

The case before the Court involved Mississippi's Gestational Age Act, which prohibited abortions after 15 weeks except for medical emergencies or severe fetal abnormalities. The act also applied penalties, such as license suspension to abortion providers. The lawsuit had been filed on behalf of Mississippi and Jackson in federal district court. The Supreme Court granted writ to address whether all pre-viability prohibitions, not just the 15-week ban, on elective abortions are unconstitutional—in Mississippi.

Neither Roe nor Casey was mentioned in the writ for Dobbs. No matter. The Court's goal was to ban all abortions. To that end, the Court seized its opportunity to slip Alito's peevish obsession and President Trump's campaign promise into the mix. Who would notice the absence of the "new case" required to overturn a constitutional law.

When you read the excerpts of *Dobbs v. Jackson Women's Health Organization (2022)*, you will see virtually nothing about Dobbs. Everything is about Roe. As a matter of fact, if you research any website talking about Dobbs, the text is packed with arguments for overturning Roe and Casey. However, neither Roe nor Casey is not called out by name in the writ for judicial review in this particular abortion case.

The Court used the assumptive closing to sell us its bill of goods.

The *Indeed Career Guide*[25] defines the assumptive closing as, "…a technique that salespeople use to encourage prospective buyers to make a purchase. It involves assuming that the customer has already agreed to make a purchase before they've explicitly done so." Under protest, the majority of voices in the nation objected to what the Court was selling us, under the color of law. No one questioned the validity of the Court's action. The majority of justices surely knew they were pulling a fast one. Didn't matter. Their president had spoken, and the Court complied. In the meantime, the American people assumed that the Court was acting in good faith and within the law.

The Court made an ass of you and me and a nation of folk who believe in law and order.

As a country, we had been primed to believe that the Supreme Court would overturn Roe V. Wade as soon as the Court had amassed its majority of Roe foes. Trump said that was his goal. We "assumed" that the Court would, of course, act appropriately.

The Trump-appointed justices did a bait-and-switch on the issue. They had led their respective confirmation committees to believe they were with the country on Roe. As a nation, we *assumed* the Court had acted within established practices. It had not. The Court had seized a convenient opportunity to succeed behind our backs.

How is constitutional law changed?

The Dobbs case was not a new case about Roe or Casey. There was no Roe v. anyone submitted from a lower court because the majority of the country favors legal and safe abortions. However, waiting for a writ to review an objection to a Roe decision would be equal to waiting for a snowstorm in Florida.

So, in. my view, the Court abused its authority, and its abuse has killed and maimed hundreds of women.

On another legal point, in all cases coming before any court, the plaintiffs must have "standing." FindLaw says that, "In order to have standing to bring suit in federal court, the plaintiff must have suffered an 'injury in fact.' This means the injury must have been caused in some way by the actions of the defendant, and the court must be able to provide a form of redress."[26]

Based upon Alito's justification for overturning Roe v. Wade and Casey v. Planned Parenthood, the Court was acting as defense for states' rights, not individual rights. Acting on its own, the absence of standing was simply a technicality that the Red Cult majority would conveniently overlook to fulfill its obligation to the president.

Judicial review was nonexistent. The Court examined nothing publicly; it just decided because it was convenient. Ba da bing! Roe v. Wade became history.

Alito compounded his maliciousness. Once he dismissed Roe v. Wade, he declared that the states had the right to decide the matter of a woman's right to an abortion. He, in his position of awesome power, led the states astray. Two constitutional amendments, the Ninth and the Fourteenth, contradict Alito's pronouncement

Nevertheless, the Red Cult legislatures wasted no time in unleashing their unconstitutional reigns of death and destruction among their constituents.

The moral eunuchs, in the thrall of their power in the Red Cult legislatures, jumped on the opportunity like snarling jackals ripping at a new carcass. The moral eunuchs in each of the Red Cult legislatures have hungrily devised ever more diabolical and deadly ways to punish a woman for being pregnant and needing an abortion.

Are Courts and Legislative Bodies Liable for Deaths due to Their Laws?

I wish I had some insight here. Inasmuch as no one is holding them accountable for breaking constitutional law, I suspect that the Good 'Ol Boys Club will claim that they have immunity from prosecution. Even though they violated constitutional law to affect the abomination, they were, gosh darn it all, doing it for the good of their state. (The majority of adults in those states disagree.)

Back to "Positivity"

The *Democracy Docket* asserts that, "While state constitutions cannot conflict with the national document, states are able to outline or clarify rights that go further than those in the federal Constitution."[27] By 2023, more than 30 states and commonwealths had done so by including abortion protections in their state constitutions.

While I might lack the sophistication to spin a web of questionable reasoning that explains the Court's handling of abortion, I do understand the transactional function of the "if this, then that" logic.

If the U.S. Constitution is silent on the abortion issue, then the state constitutions must also be silent on the matter. ("Silent" is a term used in parliamentary procedure in questions pertaining to official documents. It means that if the ruling document may say *nothing* about abortion, then the subordinate document may have nothing to say about abortion.)

The question for the public then becomes: How can the states place restrictions, implicit or explicit, on abortion when the U.S. Constitution has none?

The answer seems simple. They can't. According to the Fourteenth Amendment no state law may: assert when life begins or how many weeks into gestation that abortion is allowed; make a total-abortion ban; restrict a woman's right to make her own health-care decisions, or threaten jail time for a woman or her physician. No restrictive law of any kind may be made or enforced by any state.

Furthermore, the Ninth Amendment in the Bill of Rights protects rights "not enumerated" in the Constitution, such as abortion, marriage of any kind, birth control methods, abortion and the means to achieve an abortion, and others not specifically named. Some framers wanted to construct a list rights, but they acquiesced to this wording "The enumeration in the Constitution, of certain rights, shall not be construed to deny or disparage others retained by the people."[28]

Alito made states' rights, not individual rights, the focus of the majority decision. The devotion to states' rights is why Roe v. Wade came about in 1973. No one had questioned the constitutional authority of Texas lawmakers to institute its 15-week ban on abortions. The Roe v. Wade law reinstated the constitutional mandate of the Fourteenth Amendment, and individual states no longer had any authority to exceed the rights granted in the Constitution or to take them away. Texas's law had taken away rights; Roe returned those rights.

Again, to my simple if-this-then-that thinking, the question that should have been brought before the Court was the unconstitutionality of Texas's law against abortion. Period.

However, this is the here and the now of the 21st century. From my seat on the bus of womanhood, we are under siege. Women are being physically and emotionally violated by laws enacted by legislators who are not familiar with, or are just ignoring, constitutional law and are having an arrogant heyday at woman's expense.

Legislatures Practicing Medicine Without a License

And what about the legislative interference with a woman's right to consult with her doctor, to follow her advice, and to accept treatment, including abortion? Are these legislatures not practicing medicine without a license? By what authority does any legislative body claim the right to prohibit an individual's freedom to seek and to receive medical attention in any location for any purpose? By what authority may a state legislature restrict a licensed physician's ability to treat their patient or to threaten said physician with loss of medical license or imprisonment?

In Florida, it is a felony for anyone in the health-care professions to practice without a license. It's a felony in Texas, where some of the most heinous laws have been enacted. Are the lawmakers in Red Cult states not, in fact, making medical decisions for women, often against the advice of their licensed physicians, by enacting their life-threatening laws?

Do they not bear some measure of responsibility for the

mistreatment and maltreatment that is resulting in death, destruction of reproductive organs, and other physical maiming of hundreds of women?

Conspiracy Against Rights

Most importantly, thanks to one of the indictments of the 45th president, a significant law charged against him may well fit what the Supreme Court has done to women. The law, as applied to the 45th president, deals with his conspiring to invalidate the rights of electors. As applied to the justices, the law would deal with the potential conspiracy against a woman's constitutional right to life, liberty, and due process.

If the Conspiracy Against Rights law is good enough to indict a former president, then let's see how it fits the abominable case of the Supreme Court v. Woman Writ Large. The law, 18 U.S.C. § 242, "makes it unlawful for two or more persons to agree to injure, threaten, or intimidate a person in the United States in the free exercise or enjoyment of any right or privilege secured by the Constitution or laws of the Unites States or because of his or her having exercised such a right. Jan 17, 2023"[29]

The action of the majority on the Court has indeed injured, threatened, and intimidated women writ large, under the color of law.

Does this constitute a possible conspiracy? Well, let's consider some facts.

Alito and the other justices had testified about Roe v. Wade, under oath, before the Senate Judiciary Committee. Each testified that they believed Roe v. Wade was precedent. In his confirmation hearing, Alito told Sen. Ted Kennedy that he believed the right to privacy was settled law." He added, "So I recognize there is a right to privacy. I'm a believer in precedents. I think on the Roe case, that's about as far as I can go."[30]

In his confirmation hearing, Judge Neil Gorsuch, the 45th president's first appointment to the Court, told Sen. Chuck Grassley, under oath, that (Roe) "... is a precedent of the U.S. Supreme Court. It was reaffirmed in Casey in 1992 and in several other cases. So, a good judge will consider it as precedent of the U.S. Supreme Court worthy as treatment of precedent like any other."[31]

Judge Brett Kavanaugh, the 45th president's second appointment to the Court, said, "It is settled as a precedent of the Supreme Court, entitled the respect on principle of stare decisis. And one of the important things to keep in mind about Roe v. Wade is that it has been reaffirmed many times over the past 45 years, as you know, and prominently, most importantly, reaffirmed in Planned Parenthood v. Casey in 1992."[32] (Stare, pronounced starry, decisis is Latin for "to stand by things decided.)

Judge Amy Barrett, in her confirmation hearing, replied to a question about overturning Roe or Casey or any other case before her. "I will follow the law of stare decisis ... And I promise to do that for any issue that comes up, abortion or anything else. I'll follow the law."[33] Barrett was the 45th president's third appointment to SCOTUS.

I add here that these judges were appointed with the recommendations of the Federalist Society, of which the nominees are members. Each of the nominees, in their own time in history, was being questioned for a lifetime appointment to the Supreme Court, and they knew that Roe v. Wade was a hot-button issue for the Senate Judiciary Committee.

Several senators have said they believed that the candidates for the Court lied under oath.[34] No penalty for lying to Congress has been investigated, much less applied, however. Prevarication under oath seems to be the proverbial "nothing burger" to those entrusted with matters of law to protect us from jurisprudence malpractice.

Did these chosen ones lie under oath and, therefore, lay a veil of conspiracy against rights? Or was it merely a bait-and-switch conspiracy?

Gorsuch and Kavanaugh were firm in their answers. Barrett hedged a tad, as did Alito and Thomas in their hearings. Nonetheless, members of the committees could, and did, infer from the nominees' answers that Roe was safe in the hands of this Supreme Court.

Then, when faced with the decision to support that precedent, they forgot their pledge to the time-honored stare decisis to satisfy their personal biases and President Trump directive to get rid of Roe v. Wade. Testimony under oath, stare decisis, precedent, and women's live be damned.

Change the Premise of the Conversation

Instead of focusing so intently upon the results of the abortion laws, let's focus on the unconstitutionality of those laws. Could some crackerjack female lawyers join together to pursue the "conspiracy against rights" to bring some judicial relief for women? Or pursue the fact that the states are unconstitutionally taking away rights granted by the Ninth and Fourteenth Amendments?

I know. It's scary to challenge persons so privileged as the justices, but maybe it's time they were challenged. Or are the Supreme arbiters of jurisprudence above the laws they swore to uphold? I hear tell that no one is above the law.

The Court's decision has killed and maimed and terrorized and jeopardized the lives of tens of thousands of women. Are the lives of these women not worth the effort? Are the justices allowed to summarily remove "equal protection under law"?

Perhaps some of the 800 female law professors who objected to Justice Kavanaugh's confirmation could set an eager coterie of their best law students on the task of finding out if and how women can be vindicated. Can a lawmaker of any kind be held accountable for the heinous legislative acts that result in deliberate terrorizing, maiming, killing?

Instead of following the argument set out by the Red Cult, let's set a new precedent. Let's take the argument to the Red Cult legislatures and call them out for their lawlessness.

What can bright female legal minds do about those laws? States do not have the right to pass any of these abortion bans. Why is it happening? What can be done about it? Women are thoughtful and creative. They think outside the box. Let's turn the box on the opportunistic lawmakers.

And what about the possibility that legislators have been practicing medicine without the requisite license? They have been handing down one medically based prohibition after another. Seems like reckless endangerment to me. Or is it a new brand of abuse called "womanslaughter"? Some law must apply to those who are perpetrating this heinous, murderous abuse.

Let's fight the right battle to protect women against man's poor and pernicious judgement and need to control. Women must come together and fight for women's equal protection under Constitutional law, not man's discriminatory version of that law and hysterical view of what's happening during gestation in a woman's womb.

Are Women Too Conciliatory?

Why have women made it so easy for men to ignore the Constitution and to terrorize us with such inhumane actions? We women are not unaware, but we surely give men way too much trust and leeway in our lives. Give a man a title and the attendant power, and he gets puffed up, full of bravado, and struts.

I know, an army of people will say that I have this all wrong. And a cohort of women, fiercely loyal to their men, will take umbrage in their defense. Such is life. I have survived their rebukes for four score and six years. And, frankly, I am tired of excusing their abuses and otherwise harmful behaviors and letting them run roughshod over and through my life because I am female. Sometimes those all-powerful decision makers have trouble finding their backsides with both hands and a map. This is one of those times.

I do not *"go gentle into that good night, Old age should burn and rave at close of day; Rage, rage against the dying of the light."* I guess you could say that this old woman burns and rages at the closing of her days and rages against the dying of the light on a woman's rights and of the light on woman's God-given equality.

Next: Fetal life, not a woman's life, is the focus

Abortion Rights:
Man's Illicit Power Coup

Let's talk abortion. Abortion, as we hear about it these days, is, in my view, the red herring that diverts our attention from the patriarchy's treachery: The enactment of unconstitutional anti-abortion laws that are killing, maiming, and terrorizing women across the nation.

To be crystal clear to my reader, I shall make no apology for my brusque approach to this deadly serious topic. Man's insolent interference in a woman's personal decisions is a sham devised to control her, and controlling her, not abortion, is the focus.

These adult children in the male-dominated Red Cult state legislatures are toying with our well-being, like they are playing a cavalier game of "Mine is bigger than yours."

Michigan and friendly states (all non-Red Cult states) in the northeast and the northwest have provided abortion protections in their constitutions. The Red Cult states are busy measuring their oppressive, illegal control of women.

"We are establishing a law that says no abortion shall occur after 12 weeks," declares red Arizona.

"Ha!" redder Louisiana shouts. "We have signed a law that makes an abortion illegal after six weeks!"

Even redder Texas struts into the conversation. "We are

raising the stakes. No abortion at all. Not even for rape, incest, of the life of the mother."

Let me say right here, before we get into the contentious gist of the abortion conversation, that there are indeed female lawmakers in those Red Cult states. However, they speak in unison, as they have been so carefully taught, with their male colleagues in the legislatures. They have no opinions of their own. I have worked with countless women's organizations over my 86 years, and I recognize the women who, when asked if they to join into a project will say, "I'll have to ask Leon." The Red Cult legislatures are full of these women.

Now, back to the practice of abortion.

First, neither the word nor the deed is mentioned in Scripture. Abortion happened in Biblical time for the same reasons it happens in these times. Unwanted pregnancies. Pregnancies terminated for medical need. The methods have changed; the needs have not.

Yes, I know. "Scripture says . . ." "Scripture prohibits . . ." But you know what, Reader Friend? Those are *opinions* of what Scripture says. Not the words of God or Jesus Christ. *Opinions!* Laws founded upon prejudiced *opinions* have killed, are killing women. Prejudiced *opinions*.

Another killer is the Sixth Commandment: Thou shall not murder. The commandment once said, "Thou shalt not kill," but it was changed to "murder" in the New Testament.

Here's a buzz killer for the self-righteous religious right: God's commandments speak to you, *you* the individual reading the commandment. God's commandment does not grant a tacit license for *you* to impose your *opinion* of His commandment on anyone who disagrees with you. It behooves *you* not to murder, so that *you* don't violate the Commandment.

Nowhere in Scripture does God say that abortion is wrong or is murder. Nowhere in Scripture does Jesus say that abortion is wrong or is murder. Your *opinion* of what Scripture says should not be forced upon me or my sisters in Christ.

Speaking of opinions, in writing the Supreme Court's majority decision to overturn Roe v. Wade, Justice Samuel Alito made several statements that are opinions blatantly contrary to constitution law. His words, written as an authority entitled by privilege, are, in my view, unethical and deliberately misleading.

Full disclosure: What I write about Alito's words in the decision to overturn Roe is a full measure of my indignation and my disdain for this man. A Supreme Court Justice takes an oath to fairly mete out justice and to protect individual rights. He certainly should know better than to sanction the deliberate violation of the Bill of Rights. But, I believe he depended upon women's history and our persistent training to know our place in *his* world.

Over the centuries we have been good Christian women who have yielded to and depended upon the male authority. Alito counted on us not to question the Court's decision.

Let me say this about that: This octogenarian is questioning the actions, the words, and the intentions of the entitled, self-important Justice Samuel Alito. He will swat away my criticisms because I am female and untutored in any kind of law. Nonetheless, given my decades of experience under the prejudicial male judgement and control, I don't care what he thinks.

In this nonfiction narrative, I rebuke the Court's vengeful authority. In a crass phrase: These male bobble heads are full of corrosive horse dung.

Following is what I have learned about the villainous scam being perpetrated upon women at the pleasure of the Red Cult Master and the richly entitled justices of the Supreme Court majority. I specify the "majority" of the Court because, as compared with the minority of the Court who faithfully serve the rule of law, the majority has sacrificed the law for fealty to the Red Cult Master.

First, Alito wrote, "Eventually, in *Planned Parenthood v. Casey*, the Court revisited *Roe* ... The opinion concluded that stare decisis, which calls for prior decisions to be followed *in most instances*, required adherence to what it called Roe's 'central holding'—*that a state may not constitutionally protect fetal life before 'viability'—even if that holding was wrong.*" [35]

To be very clear, no definition for stare decisis, carries the qualifying phrase, *in most instances*. Alito added that qualifying phrase and personal misdirection to support his point. (Emphasis: the author's.)

Later he wrote, "Casey ... substituted a *new rule of uncertain origin* under which States were forbidden to adopt any regulation that imposed an *'undue burden'* on a woman's right to have an abortion ..."

The "new rule of uncertain origin" is Section 1 of the Fourteenth Amendment in the Bill of Rights. No matter how he manipulates the words, the Fourteenth Amendment is specific, of certain origin, and does not mention "undue burden."

"*No State* shall make or enforce any law which shall abridge the privileges or immunities of citizens of the United States ..."

Alito's statements, written from his seat of entitlement, erroneously and grievously granted the Red Cult legislatures implicit permission to continue their unconstitutional assault upon women's rights. The first record of the unconstitutional assault on women's rights began in 1821 in Connecticut. I repeat, loudly, the Constitution (1788) and its Supremacy Clause hold that the states have no rights not granted by the Constitution. Abortion falls within that prohibition.

The Supremacy Clause "... establishes that the federal constitution, and federal law generally, take precedence over state laws, and even state constitutions."[36] In short, the clause prohibits states from interfering with the federal government's exercise of its constitutional powers, and from assuming any functions that are exclusively entrusted to the federal government." As Alito wrote: "... the Constitution says nothing about abortion."

In 1821, the State of Connecticut codified its common law and became the first state to criminalize abortion.[37] Curiously, no men in positions of authority objected to the state's violation of constitutional law.

That historical fact was followed in 1847 with the organization of the American Medical Association (AMA)[38]. The fledgling body of physicians decided that it would determine the why and when of appropriate abortions. The fraternity, comprising a hodgepodge of medical specialties, campaigned against abortion and ended woman's place as abortion facilitators. As the fraternity eventually criminalized abortions, it also succeeded in ending the midwives place as providers of women's health care.

To this retired journalist's mind, the actions of the AMA and the state legislatures begs the question: Why did no one call attention to the gratuitous breach of constitutional law? Silly question, right? The fraternity and the patriarchy had a good thing going. They still do. They successfully adopted the unconstitutional laws under the radar. A corrosive "don't ask, don't tell" operation among the powerful men.

More questions of abusive lawlessness will surface as we continue our narrative of man's unlawful and forceful abuse of women's rights.

Questions are a journalist's stock-in-trade. I have learned to ask question after question when the information doesn't look right, sound right, or smell right. Everything about man's right to have a say in women's personal decisions stinks.

Although I am well beyond my child-bearing years, I have experienced decades of patriarchal control. Those experiences have fueled my research on the vengeful actions with which the patriarchy currently persecutes those of my gender.

For nearly 200 years, 176 to be exact, the Daddy Dearest patriarchy and its band of willful sons of the patriarchs have controlled the lives of women. This fact is especially true when it comes to critical thinking on womanly matters, such as reproductive rights. Because the current ungodly atrocity exceeds the topic of abortion, I have spent considerable time on the inconsistencies in Justice

Samuel Alito's words in his presentation of the majority's decision.

The reading was scary. From his seat of entitled jurisprudence, he made several egregiously incorrect or misleading statements that gave the Red Cult legislatures the green light to attack, with impunity, a woman's right to make her own health-care decisions.

He made these statements under condition of his oaths of federal office and of his entitled position as a Supreme Court Justice. Yes, the justices attest to two oaths of office: the standard oath to protect the Constitution and the judicial oath to administer justice fairly. (Not that either oath matters one whit to any Justice in the Red Cult majority. The majority shows no shame for its confirmed corruption and its allegiance to the Red Cult Master.) From my perspective, the Justice's words brand him as a judicial scoundrel. (*Author's note:* The revocations of Roe v. Wade and Casey v. Planned Parenthood do not appear as separate documents or decisions. They were neatly and surreptitiously folded into the Dobb's v.Jackson Women's Health Organization decision. More on this in Chapter 10.)

Among the misleading or incorrect statements, Alito wrote[39]:

1. "'A woman's right to an abortion is not implicitly protected' by the Due Process Clause of the Fourteenth Amendment to the U.S. Constitution." This statement was the first to incite the moral eunuchs in the Red Cult legislatures. This Supreme Court Justice declared that a woman is not protected by the Fourteenth Amendment. Let that sink in.
2. "For the first 185 years after the adoption of the Constitution, each state was permitted to address the issue [abortion] in accordance with the views of its citizens." Permitted, yes. Constitutionally legal, no. Oh, and translate "citizen" to "men." Only men were making decisions in 1700s and the 1800s.

3. "The Court acknowledges that States have a legitimate interest in protecting 'potential life.'" Say what?! In what legal document are the States granted this "legitimate interest" in a woman's reproductive rights? The Constitution says otherwise.

4. "Roe v. Wade was wrong in its 'central holding' that a state may not constitutionally protect feal life before viability." Roe v. Wade was spot on, but as Alito wrote, "the states objected to the restriction," hence the current Court's decision to favor the States' unconstitutional rights over a woman's constitutional rights.

5. "Roe v. Wade was wrong in its view that 'States were forbidden to adopt any regulations that imposed an 'undue burden' on a woman to have an abortion." Same song, second verse. Same rational, just as incorrect, according to the Supremacy Clause of the U.S. Constitution and the Fourteenth Amendment. Alito has been nothing, if not persistently incorrect, deceitful, and unlawful.

6. *"It is time to heed the Constitution and return the issue of abortion to the people's elected representatives."* He wrapped his tacit approval for the Red Cult legislatures to act with impunity against women in a blatant, undisguised attack upon women and their constructional rights. In Alito's own words: the Constitution says nothing about abortion or the states' rights to determine a woman's right to her health-care decisions. (Emphasis: the author's)

In a recent ruling on Donald Trump's declaration that he is immune from prosecution on charges from the January 6 insurrection and, therefore is above the law, Judge Tanya Chutkan, quoted Justice Felix Frankfurter: "If one man can be allowed to determine for himself what is law, every man can. That means first chaos, then tyranny."[40] Welcome to Justice Samuel Alito's tyranny. (Frankfurter was an Associate Justice on the Supreme Court from 1939 until 1962.)

Clearly, I have repeated information. I have done so purposefully, and I am inclined to do so again. The Court betrayed its oath of office, and women have taken the brunt of that betrayal. I have repeated these facts, and they are recorded facts, because we need to understand how man has manipulated us with misinformation and illegal actions. We have been astutely brainwashed to believe that our abiding trust in man's decisions is justified and appropriate. Man believes that in matters, such as our personal well-being, we are but simple children who need parental guidance from Daddy Dearest.

Officially, we women know only that the Supreme Court has willfully overturned 50 years of precedent in 2022. As a result of that spurious decision, the unconstitutional abortion laws have rendered us powerlessness to run our own lives, and man controls our reproductive rights as a cattle raiser controls his breeding stock. (More on this in Chapter 6.)

Alito's writing contains many more cues and key elements of propaganda that provides cover for the Red Cult legislatures to fully engage in their unconstitutional assault upon women. I call it *propaganda* because it is.

As cleverly as Alito cued the Red Cult's attack, he also contradicted himself. The one thing that Alito got right was this statement, "The Constitution makes no reference to abortion." I think he intended his words as irony, a kind of "go for it, boys," signal to the rabidly salivating Red Cult. The irony is, he reinforced the premise that because the Constitution is silent on the topic of abortion, which means that the states have absolutely no right to restrict abortion rights. Alito's word giveth and taketh away states' right to woman's health care.

The patriarchy runs amok with unconstitutional privilege and is willfully killing women and terrorizing them with their premediated repudiation of the Fourteenth Amendment.

As I said earlier, the language of the Constitution means that no life-threatening, uninformed opinions may be construed as fact and turned into deadly abortion laws. No "life begins at conception" qualifier opinion. No "life begins with the heartbeat," uninformed opinion. No "life begins with the quickening" *opinion*. No abortion bans at six weeks, 12 weeks, 15 weeks, or whatever other opinion man fabricates.

Let's end this chapter with some irony. If the states had been required to abide by the Constitution in the 1800s, Roe v. Wade would have been unnecessary.

Now, let's examine the foul bucket of SCOTUS propaganda.

The SCOTUS Propaganda

As I write this, we are but days away from celebrating the birth of Jesus and observing the holiday precepts of 14 other religions. As I finish my research and my writing of this gruesome story, I am torn between abject sorrow and palpable anger.

My heart aches for the families who mourn the loss of their beloved women—mothers, daughters, sisters, wives—who were terrorized, physically and mentally abused and died as a result of the Red Cult's cruelty. I grieve for the children who knew the love of the mother who will be missing from their holiday celebrations this year.

To the moral eunuchs in the Red Cult who have perpetrated such heinous abuses upon women, may your precious "power tool" become useless for anything other than to drain your water tank. You deserve all of that and more for sucking up to the Red Cult Master and killing women in your conceited medical overreach and causing them irreparable physical and mental harm.

I say this to the men in authority—judges, lawyers, any man in a position of power—you are sorry defenders of the rule of law. You have willingly, shamelessly condemned women to death, possible physical mutilation, and undue harm. You are complicit in that irreparable harm by failing to call out Alito's breach of constitutional law.

In case you missed his most outrageous, misleading and inappropriate words, Alito wrote, *"It is time to heed the Constitution and return the issue of abortion to the people's elected representatives,"* Heed the Constitution?! His statement violates the rule of the Constitution, and none of you said anything, ***anything,*** in opposition to his lawlessness. The Supremacy Clause in the Constitution and the Fourteenth Amendment in the Bill of Rights *prohibits*, in very clear language, the states from taking any action on any topic not expressed in those documents.

Alito declared that, with the overturning of Roe, the Constitution was devoid of any abortion reference. He, with your complicity, then declared that the states had greater authority than the Fourteenth Amendment. If I can know that his statement is inaccurate, misleading, and unethical, you, as someone who pledged your allegiance to upholding the Constitution and law in general, should know that, too. Justice Alito, writing for the Court's majority voice, is way off base in freeing the states to kill and to maim women for practicing their rights to life and liberty and due process under the Constitution.

My grandmother instilled civility and respect in my ethics. Because I honor her memory and her place in my life, I have put a lid on my "street mouth." Your willingness to cavalierly kill, maim, and terrorize women in your fealty to the Red Cult of moral eunuchs, called the patriarchy, is beyond reproach and humanity and profoundly piques my ire.

Killing women, who are the source of all life, to save the nebulous promise of life forming in a womb seems foolishly counterproductive and outrageously stupid.

A petulant, entitled Supreme Court Justice overturned a long-standing constitutional law to satisfy a 50-year itch. I quote here some of his strained and faulty reasoning from the summary of Dobbs v. Jackson Women's Health Organization (2022) decision as prepared by the National Constitution Center.

It is important that we, you and I, know how little interest the Justice had in the welfare of the women who were affected by his churlishness and how little the law he pledged to uphold means to him. His focus was on states' rights, not individual rights. I call it "moral turpitude."

I understand full well that Alito wrote the decision on behalf of the majority. Nevertheless, it is common knowledge that the fix was in to overturn Roe v. Wade. With recommendations from the Federalist Society, the President of the United States appointed the candidates who would give him what he wanted: The guaranteed demise of Roe v. Wade. Alito's writing for the majority was proforma, following the dictates of the law. The majority would sign on; that's what the majority members were expected to do. Few among the public would read the decision and, therefore, would know only what the Court wanted the public to know. So, the justices felt they were home free in their dishonorable behavior.

For reference, the Federalist Society [41] is devoted to keeping the Constitution in the dark ages. Its theme song, if it had one, would be *"Yesterday."* In fairness, this is what the society says about itself. "It is founded on the principles that the state exists to preserve freedom, that the separation of governmental powers is central to our Constitution, and that it is emphatically the province and duty of the judiciary to say what the law is, not what it should be." Do you see the irony?

However, Chief Justice Charles Evans Hughes[42], described the Constitution as a "living document" that must change and grow in concert with the changes that come before the Court. The Court disregarded that admonition as easily as they disregarded the Supremacy Clause, the Ninth Amendment, and the Fourteenth Amendment.

These next pages present substantial detail. However, the Court has carefully guarded its moral turpitude, and the press has taken the Court's ruling as the final word, without question. In contradiction to their glib explanations, I offer the observations of a female journalist. I believe that every woman and every man who cares about women needs to know just how heinously the lawmakers have manipulated the law to satisfy their prejudice and their disdain for the female human life.

Pithy and Pertinent Propaganda from the Court[60]

- *"For the first 185 years after the adoption of the Constitution, each state was permitted to address this issue in accordance with the views of its citizens."*

In his statement, Justice Alito disregarded the Supremacy Clause of our Constitution, which says that the Constitution supersedes any and all state laws. No abortion in the U.S. Constitution; no abortion in State constitutions.

- In objection to the 1973 Roe v. Wade Court, *"Roe's 'central holding'—that a State may not constitutionally protect fetal life before 'viability'—even if that holding was wrong."*

Alito was wrong in his objection to Roe. According to the Fourteenth Amendment, the states have no constitutional interest in protecting fetal life.The amendment, part of our legal history since 1866, clearly says, "No State shall make or enforce any law which shall abridge the privileges or immunities of citizens of the United States ..."

- *And in this case, 26 states have expressly asked this Court to overrule* Roe *and* Casey *and allow the States to regulate of prohibit pre-viability abortions."*

As I read the mission of the Court and the rules, such as the Judicial Review, which the Court is obliged to honor, no one gets to just "ask" the Court to overrule decisions. To bring a case before the Court, the aggrieved party in a lower court decision must file a writ of certiorari. A writ of certiorari orders the lower court to deliver its record in that case to the higher court for review.

In this case, no writ of certiorari was filed because no lower court had heard any Roe v. Anybody case. Alito and the other moral eunuchs in the Red Cult unilaterally steamrolled over every woman in the country.

- In reference to the Dobbs case, which was a legitimate X v. Y case, *"The State of Mississippi asks us to uphold the constitutionality of a law that generally prohibits an abortion after the 15th week of pregnancy ... In defending this law, the States primary argument is that we should reconsider and overrule Roe and Casey and once again allow each State to regulate abortion as its citizens wish."*

I read Dobbs. I did not see any wording that supported Alito's contention. The State's primary argument was Dobbs v. Jackson Women's Health Organization. Alito's wording "... In defending this law, the *States* primary argument is ..." The use of the plural "states" tells me that Alito was yielding to the 26 states that "asked" the Court to overturn Roe, not to the state of Mississippi.

The case before the Court was confined to Mississippi. The words Roe and Casey do not appear in the case. Hello? Once again I say, "Do you not recall the most famous constitutional rule of all, the Fourteenth Amendment?" Justice Alito, you and the Red Cult Supremes know the Constitution. Contrary to your bias, the states *do not* get "to regulate abortion as its citizens [men] wish."

- *"Until the latter part of the 20th century, such a right [to abortion] was entirely unknown in American law. Indeed, when the Fourteenth Amendment was adopted, three quarters of the States made abortion a crime."*

Yes sir, they darn well did that, in a blatant rebuke of the Supremacy Clause which I briefly restate: "States cannot make any law not first made in the name of the Constitution." Furthermore, until the time the Constitution became law and man was given a title and, therefore, the "right" to control a woman's behavior, abortion had been practiced since the beginning of time. This, to my way of thinking, meets Alito's criterion that, "... *rights that are not mentioned in the Constitution ... must be deeply rooted in this nation's history and tradition"* and *"implicit in the concept of ordered liberty."*

Justice Alito, I have to ask, "If abortion were not deeply rooted in our history, why would antiabortion laws have been necessary before the Constitution was adopted and men needed to control women's birthright?

Because four of the five justices who overturned Roe are not women, they probably were not interested to know that abortion has been a part of our history for as long as we have been recording history. The majority's "inescapable conclusion" is born of their male entitlement.

Additionally, few rights–life, liberty, due process among them, are mentioned in the Constitution. The framers of the Constitution decided that it would be too cumbersome and restrictive to enumerate a list of rights. Instead, the framers settled on the Ninth Amendment, which says, "The enumeration in the Constitution, of certain rights, shall not be construed to deny or disparage others retained by the people."

The Annenberg Classroom explains further, "Because the rights protected by the Ninth Amendment are not specified, they are referred to as 'unenumerated.' The Supreme Court has found that unenumerated rights include such important rights as the right to travel, the right to vote, the right to keep personal matters private and to make important decisions about one's health care or body." [43]

- "Roe *was egregiously wrong from the start ... and the decision has had damaging consequences.*"

This is a questionable, biased conclusion. Quasi-religious groups have complained, but complaining does not constitute "damaging consequences." Damaging consequences are what women are experiencing under this Court's abominable decision. Roe v. Wade had rightfully transferred the unlawful control of abortion from the States to the lawful control of women. Roe v. Wade gave women equal protection under established constitutional law.

Heaven forbid!

- *"Neither Roe nor Casey saw fit to invoke this theory (equal protection under the Fourteenth Amendment) and it is squarely foreclosed by our precedents, which establish that a state's regulation of abortion is not a sex-based classification ..."*

If the action against abortion is not sex-based, what, in the name of reason, is it? Men don't have abortions. Please note, too, that precedent matters when the male-dominated courts deem it to matter. The precedent that allows abortion was "wrongly" established. I detect a double standard favoring the decisions of the male-dominated lawmakers, who have a vested interest in banning abortion.

- And as the Court has stated, the *"goal of preventing abortion" does not constitute "invidiously discriminatory animus' against women ..."*

Are you freaking kidding me?! Just what do the entitled justices call it? For the record, the word "invidious" is a sickening, demeaning word that means, among other definitions, "unpleasant" and "unfair." The men making the unlawful decisions in the states do not think it unpleasant or unfair that they have made ignorant and hostile decisions on a woman's behalf. Who are these people?

- *"The Constitution makes no express reference to a right to obtain an abortion, and, therefore, those who claim that it protects such a right must show that the right is somehow implicit in the constitutional text ..."*

To bring Alito's reasoning full circle, the Constitution does not specifically say that men have the right to use Viagra. If men are constitutionally allowed an unfettered right to an artificially induced erection, then women are constitutionally granted the right to unfettered health-care abortions. To put a finer point on the argument, if men can legitimately and artificially "get it up," women should be able to legitimately and safely "get it out."

- *"On the contrary, an unbroken tradition of prohibiting abortions on pain of criminal punishment persisted from the early days of common law until 1973 (Roe v. Wade)."*

Yes, indeed. That is a true statement. At least since 1845. In that year, the male bastions of lawmakers welcomed Texas as our 28th state, and allowed it to retain its unconstitutional laws, in contravention to the U.S. Constitution. We adapted our national attitude on abortion to Texas's way of thinking. Since then, we have allowed states, in a breach of constitutional law, to criminalize abortion and punish women. This has been done, as I reported in Chapter 7, in the name of controlling man's breeding stock to preserve the white patriarchy.

From the first unconstitutional abortion laws, man has considered women as breeding stock to be controlled to protect the white patriarchy.

"These (abortion) laws weren't so much preventative as they were disciplinary ... This is about making an example, especially an example of white women and ... disciplining white fertility."[44]

— Lina-Maria Murillo. Historian at the University of Iowa
who has studied abortion laws in Texas and Mexico

"In Texas, a slave state with a large Mexican population, these racial concerns were front and center ... Maintaining white birth rates was seen, at that time, as an essential part of maintaining white power in the state."[45]

— Lina-Maria Murillo. Historian at the University of Iowa
who has studied abortion laws in Texas and Mexico

"The thought was that with the abortion laws as they stood, the racial stock of the U.S. was going to decline ... Because the wrong people were going to be having more kids and the right people were going to be having fewer kids.[46]

— Mary Ziegler, Florida State University College of Law,
a legal historian focusing on abortion

Man Reduced Women to "Breeding Stock"

I have purposely changed the structure of this chapter's opening page. I want you to feel the full impact of my research on the abortion laws in Texas. They represent the primitive beliefs, past and present, of the male lawmakers. Their attitudes about abortion are formed by their fear of losing the white patriarchy. The audacity of men to appropriate control of our minds and our bodies to ensure their supremacy is loathsome.

Have disbelief and outrage in learning that the abortion laws were originally enacted to control us women as breeding stock to perpetuate the patriarchy begun to stir in your mind?!

If you dismissed that thought with an, "Oh, that was then, this is now," think again. Regrettably, man's attention to birthing the right color of kids to maintain white power continues today. Republicans have accused Democrats of manipulating immigration laws to increase the nonwhite population and, thereby tilt the balance of power away from white males. The Republicans are terrorized by the statistics that one day, in the not-too-distant future, the white male will be just another plurality, with no particular position of power.

Justice Clarence Thomas said, upon the overturning of Roe v. Wade, that other precedents, such as interracial marriages and the right to contraception should be reversed as well. Implying that interracial unions, such as his, dilute the whiteness of our population of our nation. The Red Cult Master also believes that our whiteness must be preserved, and he has plans to ensure that expectation if he returns to office in 2024.

Texas's ruthless laws, codified in 1857, have a long and punitive history based upon woman's position as breeding stock. The vile decisions, the likes of which the men of power have recently forced upon Kate Cox[47], have a long, obscene, and unconstitutional background. Ms. Cox sought and was granted an exception to Texas's abortion law to save her life and her continued ability to have children.

Powerful men in positions of powerful decision-making authority have, for instance, imposed their unlicensed medical opinions and denied Ms. Cox's the life-saving procedure. In their esteemed positions as hack-and-quack medical professionals, they decided that her condition did not qualify her for the any exception to the law. She fled the state of Texas in order to save her life.

Then we have Brittany Watts of Ohio who experienced the spontaneous abortion of her nonviable fetus at home. The fetus was expelled into the toilet. Watts was arrested and faced prison time if she were found guilty of "abuse of a corpse." The charge is generally applied to experimentation, not to a spontaneous medical event. A grand jury declined to indict her.[48]

No matter in which state man's conceited and insupportable disregard for constitutional law begins, his arrogance and lawlessness are killing, maiming, and terrorizing women in the name of protecting "potential" life. To sacrifice a well-founded life to save a "maybe" is supremely justifiable in man's mind.

I am putting this chapter on man's odious and illicit coup in a timeline sequence so that the way in which the male-dominated lawmakers have manipulated the laws against our rights are clear and totally unambiguous.

One fact you may notice is, we have had the Supremacy

Clause from the beginning of the Union and, eventually, we gained the Ninth and Fourteenth amendments. According to the men in power, none of these constitutional laws has any bearing on a woman's protection under on their right to act as they wish. Man's control of his women is absolute. Constitutional law be damned.

Unconstitutional Abortion Laws by the Numbers[49]

- The U.S. Constitution was ratified in 1787 and became law in 1788. The Constitution contained, and still does, the Supremacy Clause which made clear that any and all federal laws superseded any and all state laws. A state may expand rights, but it may not restrict or take away rights not limited in the Constitution.

- In 1791, the first 10 amendments to the Constitution were ratified and became known as the U.S. Bill of Rights.

- In 1821, in violation of the Supremacy Clause and the Bill of Rights, the state of Connecticut, one of the 13 original states, codified its abortion laws. In doing so, the state also criminalized all abortions. In 1990, Connecticut changed its viewpoint and enshrined the right to an abortion in its state constitution.

- In 1846, Texas became the 28th state admitted to the United States. In contravention of the U.S. Constitution and its Supremacy Clause, the male-dominated body of lawmakers welcomed the state of Texas and its abortion laws into our union. The state was not required to abide by the laws of the U.S. Constitution, the law of the land. The men in charge of governmental decisions didn't care. Women's God-given right to give birth belonged to the patriarchy.

- In 1847, the American Medical Association (AMA) was formed in Philadelphia, PA. In violation of the Constitution, the fraternity, comprising a hodgepodge of medical specialties, campaigned against abortion and ended woman's place as abortion facilitators. The fraternity eventually succeeded in criminalizing abortions.

- In 1853, the Texas legislature authorized the creation of the Medical Association of Texas, another fraternity that was granted the power to interfere in women's decisions on their reproductive rights, in contravention to the Constitution.

- In 1868, the lawmakers incorporated the Fourteenth Amendment into the U.S. Bill of Rights. That amendment reinforced and further delineated the tenets of the Supremacy Clause and the Ninth Amendment.

- In 2022, the Supreme Court summarily overturned 50 years of precedent and eliminated women's equal protection under the law. In contravention to the Fourteenth Amendment, the majority on the Court declared that the several and individual states had the right to enact abortion laws.

Now, in contravention to the Supremacy Clause, and the Ninth and the Fourteenth amendments, the states that are controlled by the Republican Party are spewing illegal and deadly abortion laws with astounding efficiency.

Again, in violation of the Supremacy Clause and those same amendments, the willful and entitled men are proposing a total ban on abortions, man's total control of woman's body and health decisions. No exceptions whatsoever.

The irony here is that the men adopting the unconstitutional laws have everyone focused on the symptom of the problem: the loss of constitutional rights. That ruse keeps our attention permanently diverted from the rot that causes the loss of abortion rights: The deceitful, unconstitutional laws that protect the patriarchy.

Ironically, the white patriarchy has been doomed for decades. However, because they live in their male-centered world and ignore pertinent information about reality, men have missed the memo. Here is a synopsis of the research on the white majority, as reported by *The Conversation*[50] in 2019.

"America is on its way to becoming predominately nonwhite … the decline of the white share of the U.S. population could result in the shifting of racial boundaries to assign whiteness to some people of color so as to the bolster the white numbers … But any future changes cannot override demography. The U.S. will *never* be white again." (Emphasis: the author's)

The decline in the white population has been occurring since the 1950s. The population comprised about 90% Whites then; in 2018, only 60% of the population was white. The researchers report that by about 2044, the United States will be a majority-minority country. "Majority-minority" refers to a subdivision (nation or state) in which one or more racial, ethnic, and/or religious minorities make up a majority of the local population. In this case, the term refers to the populations of individual states.

In 2002, six states—Hawaii, the District of Columbia, California, New Mexico, Texas, and Nevada—reflected populations that were a majority of nonwhites. (Which explains why the white male Texans especially are clutching their family jewels.) In 2018, the populations of 14 states were below 60%. The six already mentioned fell below 50% white folk. The eight other states are: Maryland, Georgia, Florida, Arizona, New York, New Jersey, Mississippi, and Louisiana.

The Conversation reports, "In 2015, for the first time, there were more white deaths in the U.S. than white births. Indeed, as of 2016, in 26 states whites were dying faster that they were being born."

To be more specific, the National Centers for Health Statistics reports "that in 2021, 1,205 women died of maternal causes in the United States compared with 861 in 2020 and 754 in 2019. The maternal mortality rate for 2021 was 32.9 deaths per 100,000 live births, compared with a rate of 23.8 in 2020 and 20.1 in 2019."[48] These figures have nothing to do with abortions. Those women died as the result of giving birth. The World Health Organization defines a maternal death as "the death of a woman while pregnant or within 42 days of termination of pregnancy, irrespective of the duration and the site of the pregnancy, from any cause related to or aggravated by the pregnancy or its management, but not from accidental or incidental causes."[51]

As a historical note, the formation of the Constitution and the Bill of Rights, designed to protect us all, had their opposition. The Federalists—George Washington, Benjamin Franklin, and James Madison, among others—believed that a strong Constitution was all that was necessary to protect individual rights. A strong central government and weak state governments would do the trick.

The antifederalists—John Hancock, Patrick Henry, and George Mason, among others—disagreed. They believed that the Constitution was insufficient to protect individual rights. They wanted the power in the states, not the central government, to avoid tyranny. The antifederalists gave us the Bill of Rights.[52]

Regardless of the supposed "protections," tyranny reigns.

When it comes to women's rights, neither document protects us. Man uses the Constitution as he uses Bible. He restates the laws and the precepts in each as convenient tools to control women.

The men in power have assumed control of their treasured breeding stock. They have enslaved women as the plantation owners enslaved their women. In contravention to the U.S. Constitution, the Red Cult majority has wrongfully conferred the rights that states relish. In doing so, the majority justices repudiated their oath to protect the rights of individuals in favor of protecting imaginary states' rights.

I end this chapter with Judge Tanya Chutkan's recent succinct and powerful statement in United States of America v. Donald J. Trump.[53]

- *"By definition, the President's duty to take Care that the Laws be faithfully executed' does not grant special latitude to violate them.*

- *"As the Supreme Court has stated, that principle must govern citizens and officials alike: No officer of the law may set that law at defiance with impunity.*

- *"All officers of the government, from the highest to the lowest, are creatures of the law and are bound to obey it. It is the only supreme power in our system of government, and every man who by accepting office participates in its functions is only the more strongly bound to submit to that supremacy, and to observe the limitations which it imposes upon the exercise of the authority it gives."* (Emphasis: the author's)

Now, a word about reclaiming our bodies.

Reclaiming Our Bodies

"What causes unwanted pregnancies and abortions? Men enjoying sex and having irresponsible ejaculations."[54]

This chapter is a no-holds-barred message—woman to woman. You may not like part of it, but I make no apology for saying that boys/men have sucker punched us since we were teenagers. More to the point, they have stuck it to us, with our permission, and it hasn't always been fun.

And now, the patriarchy, in its passion to control us, has the organizations who represent women's rights chasing the wrong dog in the hunt for abortion rights. Yes, the antiabortion laws, all unconstitutional laws, I might add, are killing and maiming women and terrorizing them, in servitude to man's need to control women.

This chapter is about women, legitimate members of our country and humanity, reclaiming our rights as guaranteed under the Fourteenth Amendment. It will take some courage. In the name of pleasing our men, as our mommas said we must do, we have sold our souls and our bodies. We have sacrificed ourselves to unwanted pregnancies, spontaneous abortions, pain and suffering in the name of birth control.

We have bent to the male ego and accepted his lack of responsibility in the sex act and lack of respect for us as his sex partner.

And here we are again. Men screwing us in abject enactment of unconstitutional laws that are killing, maiming, and terrorizing us. We fail to claim esteem for ourselves.

Before I move on to a man's responsibility for unwanted pregnancies, I'm going to deal with the unconstitutional antiabortion laws right up front. I want you to be very aware of how lawmakers are openly violating the United States Constitution, and the men in charge do not care. The effect of these actions upon women is nothing to any of them.

We have personal history to show that men generally do not care about us in bed. Their wants are paramount. Neither do men protects with the same system of laws that protect them.

As an octogenarian who grew up in the dark age of "unenlightenment," it is important to me that you know more than I did when I was your age and having babies, despite my planning.

Nevertheless, as angry as their disregard for a woman's rights makes me, this whole "unwanted pregnancy" thing, the need for an abortion, begins with us, you and me.

Through the ages and to our detriment, we have allowed men to call the shots when it comes to sex. From our encounters with youthful experimental sex to sex in marriage, we have remained silent. When we have granted "our man" the right to enter our vaginas unprotected, we have relinquished our dignity, our future, and our right to decide whether we want to have a baby.

Here's a quote from a book I unabashedly endorse: "We need to focus on men and stopping irresponsible ejaculations. Everything else—reducing unwanted pregnancies, reducing abortions—follows from this critical focus."

The book of which I speak has a shocking red-orange cover, a shockingly essential message, and an equally shocking title: *Ejaculate Responsibly: A Whole New Way to Think About Abortion.* On the back cover it says, "Why abortion is a men's issue."[55] That statement brought my brain to attention. Much of what I write in this chapter comes from that book, with additional research on the main points. A journalist does not accept only one viewpoint.

The author, Gabrielle Blair, wrote that, "We've put the burden of pregnancy on the person who is fertile for 24 hours a *month*, instead of the person who is fertile 24 hours a *day*, every day of their life."[56] Think about that for a minute. A woman can have a single pregnancy in a year. Man on the other hand, being irresponsible in his ejaculation can make 365 babies, or more, in that same year.

In a few well-written pages, Blair helped me to understand how I ended up with babies I had not planned on. I was ignorant of how undependable my method was for determining my fertility cycle. Actually, the birth-control information available in the 1950s was sketchy and mostly the fabric of old-wives tales.

Right here and now, my reader friend, I urge you to acquire a copy of *Ejaculate Responsibly*. And a copy for your daughter. And a copy for your sister. A copy for any woman of child-bearing age about whom you care. The book points up how a man's irresponsible attitude toward sex and our complicity in his precious sexual freedom with our bodies have seriously altered our lives with many unexpected, unwanted, and sometimes dangerous pregnancies.

Blair's startling nonfiction narrative provides critical information about our fertility cycle and equips the reader with an understanding of how the miscalculations occur. Her narrative also gives us permission to put prevent unwanted pregnancies and, therefore, reduce the need for abortions landed on our doorsteps.

I am a prime example of a woman who was ignorant about how her body worked. I knew how I got pregnant; I didn't know why it occurred. I was following the prescribed routine that involved the 28-day-cycle.

Sixty-five years ago, we absolutely did not share information about intimate topics. We generally didn't talk about irregular menstrual cycles. Few of us, if any, had any sex education or any instruction in how our bodies functioned. We just had sex, which, most frequently, resulted in babies.

As a result, over a period of 15 years, I had eight pregnancies, which resulted in five live births and three spontaneous abortions (miscarriages). I didn't necessarily want those pregnancies, but they were accepted. My husband and I wanted a family. No matter how carefully we tried to space our children, the pregnancies surprised us.

Of course, like most women then, I knew about the 28-day cycle, and how a woman *should* be able to magically determine when she would be fertile. That was the extent of my knowledge. That was about all we knew then or know now.

My gynecologists, all men in my day, never explained anything. They performed the routine vaginal exam, which confirmed what I already knew. A baby was imminent.

Some basic sex education in school would have benefitted us all, but my experience as a reporter revealed that fathers were adamant about their innocent little girls learning about their bodies and reproduction in sex-education classes in school. Whenever that topic came up in school board meetings, the fathers were most adamant. Only heaven knew, they argued, what mischief would result from talking about sex in school. These men were speaking from their history. They worried that their freedom to have their way with the local girls would be curtailed. So the young women of the era, of any era, were left with the mythology of the 28-day cycle

One reading through Blair's simple and well-written book, and I understood why I had those eight pregnancies. What I learned from her straight-forward information could have saved me the grief of those miscarriages. Hopefully, the information will save you, or someone you love, from an unwanted or unexpected pregnancy.

From the beginning of time, our ignorance of our gynecological function has resulted in countless, accepted-but-unwanted pregnancies. Or unwanted pregnancies that ended by a brutal abortion—spontaneous or planned. Rarely, if ever, did a pregnancy occur as planned. If a husband and wife agreed that they wanted children, that was about all the planning that was going to occur.

Here is a synopsis of the high points in our ignorance.[57]

1. A woman has a fertility window of about 12 to 24 hours, once a month. She does not, however, have any reliable idea of when ovulation, the fertile time, will occur.
2. That window of fertility is a moveable event. The 28-day cycle has little to do with trying to determine a woman's time of ovulation. Neither does her temperature. A Ouija board could be just as reliable.
3. A man is fertile 24 hours a day, seven days a week, 365 days a year, until he dies. He knows what's going to happen and when. No excuses for him.
4. His little swimmers, all 180 million of them, in his eight-second burst of manly pleasure, are heat seeking missiles for five days. Five days!
5. Because a woman has no control over her window of fertility and man has control over when and where he deposits his swimmers, unprotected sex invariably ends in an unwanted pregnancy. No matter how carefully a couple might plan, a five-day margin of error almost guarantees failure.

How old were you when you learned that information? Most of us have not known. Pertinent information in every life-altering situation is everything.

So, what now? Now comes the tough part. The time for courage and decision-making. One courageous woman at a time. This is your time.

You can start by asking one of the most significant questions you will ever ask yourself before you engage in sex. Are you willing to risk a pregnancy at this time in your life?

Have you and your husband decided to start a family? If you haven't, then it's time to talk about contraception. Your discussion is particularly important because if you don't want children and you miscalculate in the game of unprotected baby-making roulette, you may win the lifetime job called motherhood. The man always walks away to play another day.

(Caveat: I make no judgment of the value of motherhood here. As I said, I have five children. If you're ready to start a family, great. If not, then you have an important decision to make.)

If you and your boyfriend are sexually active, the same initial question applies. Do you, a young woman with her hopes and dreams ahead of her, want to risk having a baby at this time in your life? If not, then contraception is *must* conversation. Unless, of course, you are okay with the probability of being a single mom for at least 18 years. Abortion no longer is a safe option, thanks to the barbaric unconstitutional antiabortion laws currently being passed.

Don't think for a minute that your pregnancy will necessarily "hook" your Mister Right into marrying you because he's going to be daddy. Biologically, yes, he will be your baby's daddy. However, based upon decades of hearing how a man became angry because his sex mate "took seriously what he poked into her in fun," there is no guarantee. (Men love to make light humor at our expense, raising questions of *our* naiveté and sensitivity.) The announcement of a pregnancy frequently ends with statements like: "I don't want any damn baby!" "Why weren't *you* more careful?" "What were *you* thinking?" And, the "It wasn't my fault" escape question, "Who else have you been sleeping with?"

Because we women have acquiesced to our man's whining about how using a condom destroys his feeling of manliness and how intercourse doesn't feel right wearing a condom, we have assumed all responsibility—emotional, physical, and financial—for protecting our wellbeing.

So that our man can have his fun, preserve his sense of manliness, and walk away feeling good about himself, we accept the continual expense and the ugly, painful, and often debilitating side effects of the pill or the IUD or the injection.

Think about this for a minute. While he goes about his days and nights, free as a stray dog, you are experiencing one or more of these side effects: depression, fatigue, headaches, insomnia, mood swings, nausea, breast pain, vomiting, weight gain, acne, and bloating. The more deadly side effects that you may experience while you pledge yourself to preserving your man's pride and the holiness of his power tool are blood clots, heart attack, high blood pressure, liver cancer, and stroke.

How noble of you to sacrifice your health and wellbeing for his satisfaction and his pride. Is this what you want for the rest of our childbearing days?

If you opt for an intrauterine device (IUD), you may experience double trouble. Not only is it probable that you will experience the side effects from the list above, but you also will bear the financial cost and the possibility of monstrous periods. All to protect your man's pride.

And, now, the male-dominated pharmaceutical companies are promoting yet another drug to "give me control." Sounds good in principle. Still, the product is but another way to persuade women that they are strong and taking "control." Nothing has changed. Woman continues to take full physical, mental and financial responsibility for the sperm donor's irresponsibility. She can happily alter her ovulation and screw up her natural rhythms so her man can continue to feel "manly," without a condom. No matter how much it costs us, we must sacrifice so that our sex partner can continue to be disrespectful and irresponsible.

The message in all of this is: if we women want to be sexually active, "This is the price we must pay. Suck it up because we have given our pride over to our man."[58] Or we could stand firm in our decision to put ourselves first. We could be resolute in our expectation that our man will respect us and be responsible to our relationship. Tell him to put a rubber sock on it and respect you and your decision to avoid a pregnancy, or forget the fun.

For the record, I am well aware that men often deliver more than abusive words when his playtime is threatened or playtime results in a child. Men act with impunity and often brutally; women hesitate to act at all. Be aware that men are equally as vulnerable as women. Just in a more intimate and sharply painful way. (More later)

Don't want a baby, or the second or third baby? Then be proactive and selfish enough to put your health, your future ahead of his wheedling and whining, his disrespect for you.

One of my early assignments as a reporter was to cover a school board meeting about introducing sex education into the high-school curriculum. About an hour into the meeting, the demeanor devolved into a shouting match. The meeting went from a reasonable-but-intense discussion to a mother's rant about how *her* son's reputation and future were *not* going to be ruined by some *girl* with *loose morals*. A baby was the girl's problem, not her precious son's.

Other women accused some young men in town of sowing their wild oats and not being held responsible for their irresponsible behavior. As you can imagine, the meeting ended on a cantankerous note.

Through my years as a journalist, that meeting was not the last time I heard more than one momma rant about her boy's life being ruined by a girl with questionable morals. The male's behavior never is questioned, only the female's "loose morals." The use of condoms was never mentioned, either. That would certainly signify a permission to continue the illicit behavior.

If you are a Catholic, as I am, contraception always is a concern. You worry about being ostracized for violating the church's rigid contraception rules. Here's something you need to know. As with the topic of abortion, the Bible says *nothing* against contraception. The rules against contraception in the Catholic church are man-made, not God-made.

The church's hierarchy, the bishopric (an apt name) has interpreted or extrapolated select Scripture to satisfy their need to make contraception of any kind a sin against creation. Among those passages are, "Go forth and multiply." Clearly, we humans have done as we were directed by God. Our world population continues to grow, and we don't need any gratuitous admonitions from the church.

For the record: Neither God nor Jesus uttered a word for or against contraception. Neither does Scripture insist that it is a woman's obligation to have a baby every year. Only man's interpretation of select scriptures insists upon *her* fidelity to the church and its baby-making rules.

As I reported, Blair's unambiguous explanations give evidence as to why the Catholic's long-touted rhythm method of birth control does not work.

The self-righteous men in the Catholic church praise their women for producing 12, 13, 17 babies over a woman's lifetime. It's a "blessing from God," they say, smiling beatifically as they literally pat the woman on the head.

From this Catholic woman's viewpoint, the church-imposed obligation to procreate, like the abortion bans, puts man in the eternal control over woman. A woman's failing health or her declining financial ability to care for her brood are of no concern to the church or to the bishopric.

Exercising a little Biblical extrapolation of my own, Romans 14:12 applies to the notion that contraception is okay. "Each of us will render an account for himself to God." On a more positive note, the Book of Solomon gives a healthy account of sex for pleasure, not just procreation. The Catholic church isn't into pleasure much; it's into popping out babies to provide future priests, for the glory of God. Kind of like abortion bans protect the white patriarchy. The control is just as insidious.

Passages in 1 Corinthians 10:23-33 puts the business of everything we do, including contraception, into the framework of the New Testament. The New Testament, the premise of which we are to observe, is based upon the promise that Christ's death on the cross fulfilled all laws of the Old Testament, paid for our sins with his blood, and gave mankind free will.

We can do anything so long as we are glorifying God with

our actions. That means choosing what is right, as God directs us, for our own lives. However, there is a caveat. As the passage from Romans says, we will be expected to give an accounting of our decisions when we come to our judgment day.

Which means, putting it politely, the men in the Catholic church have nothing to say because, by New Testament expectations, deciding to have a baby is a choice that belongs to the individual couple. One other Scripture, from my perspective, ties a knot in the Catholic church's rope that binds women to man's edict. "There is only one lawgiver and judge, he who is able to save and to destroy. But who are you to judge your neighbor?" (James 4:12). There is only one lawgiver, and he is not the Pope or the bishopric in Rome.

That a couple must rely solely upon the rhythm method of birth control is *church doctrine* from the male dominated church, not a God rule found in Scripture.

A final thought from Blair's book. An excerpt from *The 8th List of Shit That Made Me a Feminist.*[59]

> *Patriarchy teaches us that sex, for women, is a giveaway, while for men it is a takeaway.*
>
> *She saves herself, gives herself to the right one, and then her virginity is lost. In this equation, there is nothing in sex that's for her to* take. *Whereas he* takes *and SCORES and there is nothing in sex for him to* give. *When her mind in programmed to give, she struggles to say 'no.' When his mind is programmed to take he struggles to accept 'no.'"*

We must not forget about pregnancies from rape
This chapter, *Reclaiming Our Bodies*, has focused on preventing pregnancies by taking responsibility to hold the other half of the

baby-making duo equally as responsible. However, we cannot protect ourselves from rape. An angry man will take what he believes is his, and rape is about anger and power over the person the man hates and resents.

The male-dominated legislatures and courts are taking away sex-abuse protections and a woman's right to determine her normal reproductive choices, those resulting from unexpected fetal abnormalities, and sexual abuse. Additionally, the moral eunuchs on the Supreme Court are planning to take away a woman's right to contraceptives, which may well mean all other means of birth control.

The Court is not, however, curtailing any of the drugs that overcome erectile dysfunction. The advertisements for a cheaper version of Viagra, mail-order Viagra, and the new-and-improved Cialis-plus are never ending.

But have you seen any advertisements about antirape devices? I have not, and I notice the unusual. Nevertheless, those devices are out there and have been for many years. Here are two trustworthy websites to get you started in your research:

- https://www.psychologytoday.com/us/blog/the-body-blog/201704/10-best-tech-devices-prevent-rape
- https://www.thehealthsite.com/photo-gallery/diseases-conditions-anti-rape-devices-every-woman-should-know-about-po0316-376146/anti-rape-devices-376156/.

The point here is, antirape devices have been available from the days of the chastity belts of the really old days. And like Viagra, there are newer, improved, and cheaper versions, but, unlike Viagra, these devices are not marketed to the public in this country. Male-dominated advertising agencies control the flow of information.

Seems to me that any antirape device would be a profitable venture. Nevertheless, it remains quite unlikely that any male-dominated development company (which most are) or venture capitalist (of which most are male) is going to go out on a limb to invest in and promote a product that will protect women from man's time-honored hate-powered abuse of women. A woman with money to invest in women could make a bundle in the rape-prevention business.

Anyway, this part of my research resulted from a post on my Face Book account that featured an antirape device that makes the other devices look like a birthday party favor by comparison. And its effect on the rapist would revolutionize the rape landscape. Men would think twice about dropping a date-rape drug into a likely sex prospect's drink. Or a bunch of fraternity brats would be less likely to engage in gang rape. Their legacy entitlements would not protect them from their public embarrassment that this particular antirape device would unerringly inflict.

Furthermore, once the word about this device got out on the street, even the angriest of men on power trips might hesitate to expose himself to pain and being caught with his pants down, with no place to hide.

The device is the Rape-aXe, developed in 2010. It is a soft latex sheath that a woman can insert into and remove from her vagina as easily as she inserts and removes a tampon. This female latex condom is lined with rows of serrated "teeth" that latch onto the rapist's penis with his first angry, forceful thrust. When, in surprise and pain, the rapist pulls out, the hungry condom comes with his penis. And he cannot remove the device without considerable damage to his precious member. The device must be removed by a medical clinician.

"It hurts, he cannot pee and walk when it's on," says the inventor, Dr. Sonnett Ehlers. "If he tries to remove it, it will clasp even tighter … however, it doesn't break the skin, and there's no danger of fluid exposure."[60]

Dr. Ehlers, who had worked with many rape victims, invented the device in response to a rape victim. Ehlers was on call one night four decades ago, when a devastated rape victim walked in. Her eyes were lifeless, like she was a breathing corpse," Ehlers recalls.

"She looked at me and said, 'If only I had teeth down there,'" recalled Ehlers, who was a 20-year-old medical researcher at the time. "I promised her I'd do something to help people like her one day." And, so, she did.

In a twist of irony, females in positions of authority and influence downplay the antirape devices, because the devices make women "slaves to their protection" and "The devices remind women of their vulnerability." Whose interests are they promoting?

Funniest darn thing. For all my years as a woman who worried about her safety anytime she was in an iffy situation, I have been very aware of my vulnerability to men who were bigger and stronger than I. I think having the protection of an antirape device would have made me feel a whole lot less vulnerable as a reporter in a man's world.

The next chapter may be useful in planning to protect yourself against your man's objection to thwarting his passion for abusing you at your expense.

We Are Equals in Our Vulnerability

"I've been thinking, Arrabiato." The olive-skinned woman runs her fingers through her glossy dark hair next to her ear, as she speaks to her husband.

"That must have worn you out." He sneers, fiddling with the TV remote.

"You know how you're always telling me that you love me, but you beat on me because I irritate you?" She dunks her tea bag in her nearly empty, chipped white mug. "I'm think I'm tired of being your punching bag."

"Yeah? And what are you going to do about it?" He looks at her, skeptically. "There's no way you can stand up to me," he says. He makes a disdainful hiss as he waves his hand, dismissively. Arrabiato leans back and lays his right ankle over his left knee, a show of contempt.

Fortuna stands up, bracing her fingers on the tabletop. She walks to the kitchen sink. She walks slowly, gingerly holding her left side. Her ribs still are tender from the pounding Arrabiato gave her three days ago. Her shoulders ache. Her forearms are bruised and tender from where she tried to defend herself. She sets the cup in the sink and throws the tea bag in the trash.

"Well? What're you gonna do? Huh?" Fortuna turns and stares at him, assessing his attitude.

"You beat me because I'm vulnerable. Easy to beat on because I'm not strong, big like you." Her crisp, angry words snap in the air. "But you are as vulnerable as me. Maybe more so."

"No way, bitch. You gonna hire someone to get me coming outta the bar? Keep me from comin' home?"

"No, Arra. Something much easier than that. I'm going to come for the boys you're so proud of." She waggles her index finger in front of him, deliberately and shakes her head slowly.

"What!? Are you crazy?" Arra lurches forward in the over-stuffed chair. "What made you think of something like that?"

"Well, you make such a big deal of how important they are. You talk about 'the boys' like they are part of the family. You're disgusting when you rub your private parts through your pants. And I see how you flinch when some guy on America's Funniest Videos gets hit in the crotch.

"And I'm tired of hurting, Arrabiato." She stands a little straighter. "Tired of explaining the bruises to my friends. The broken arm." She takes an uncertain step toward him. "Tired of making excuses for you. Tired of the looks from the doctors and nurses in the emergency room. I'm tired of every pill, every shot, every X-ray."

She braces herself on the cheap, beige Formica dinette table. They had bought the table at a garage sale when they were first married. It looks as misused as she does.

Fortuna stares squarely into her husband's eyes with a hate that matches her pain, her disgust. Last night, lying awake in pain, she swore that she would not put up with his abuse ever again.

"What's going on with you?" Fortuna had never behaved this way. "You think you're gonna take me here and now? You really are nuts." Arrabiato starts to get to his feet but thinks better of that idea and settles back into his seat. Fortuna turns toward him. Arra stiffens.

"Listen, you stupid bitch!" His voice was fearful, uncertain. "I'll knock you on your ass before you can raise your foot." He stays seated.

"Oh, I know that, Arra." She laughed, the edge of sarcasm lingering between them. "I wouldn't try anything so silly. Unless the opportunity was just right." She stops next to the table, using it as support against her thigh.

Arra was edgy. This behavior was so off. Fortuna always just took the whipping. She cried and begged, but she had never acted out like this. With each deliberate word, her voice sounded stronger, more determined.

"I know it would be foolish to go head on with you. But when you are in bed, asleep, you will be vulnerable like me. Your drinking and your exhaustion from beating on me will make you like putty in my hands."

"What are you talking about?" Arra asks, a touch of fear tightening his throat. Vulnerable in bed? What was she saying? He squirmed in his seat.

"What am I talking about? I'm talking about this." She pushes herself away from the table, straightens her posture, and stares into his soul. "The next time you want to pound on me because I irritate you, remember these words: 'I'll be waiting for you in the darkness.'

"When I am laying there, my lip busted, my eye black, the pain spreading and throbbing all through my body, I'll be waiting.

"Maybe I won't do anything the first night because I'm hurting too much. But there will be the next night, or the night after that. But there will be another night when you are drunk and vulnerable. You're always drunk. You won't know when. But I'll grab your boys and hold 'em real tight," her eyes narrow and her fingers curl into a fist. "As tight as my aching body will let me. I want you to feel what I feel. The best thing is, I don't need much strength to make you scream in pain." She clenches her fingers quickly, tightly, and grimaces. Arrabiato jerks.

"You know I'll come after you harder than ever, Fortuna. You can count on that" Arra said. "I'm not taking any shit from you or any woman. You're just a dumb bitch who's in over her head on this plan." Arra was breathing hard, fear creeping around in his body, sweat soaking his arm pits and beading on his top lip.

"Well, Arrabiato, that's where your vulnerability will equal mine. If you come for me, you can count on my visiting 'the boys' in the night again and again. With just as much love and affection as I gave 'em the first time. You won't know when, but I will visit. I promise you that." Her harsh words hissed at him. "You can't stay awake forever after wearing yourself out, beating on me.

"You will wonder when I turn over next to you. You will listen for me to fall asleep, for my breathing to change." She stood silently for a few seconds. "Hit me again, Arrabiato, and you will never have another peaceful night. You will feel what you have done to me.

"Here's something else you need to know. I am keeping a list of all my ER visits and treatments. Every bruise, every broken collar bone, everything. Times and dates. Names of hospitals and doctors. I keep the list hidden, but two friends know where to find it.

"If you kill me, or try to kill me, they will take the list to the authorities. The cops won't do anything, but the lawyer will. I also have handwritten a letter that explains how and why you pounded on me. I have handwritten it so that the authorities know that the list is authentic. I have given handwritten notes to both of my friends, so that the authorities will have a comparison.

"If you don't hear another thing I am saying Arrabiato, hear this. I am tried of being your punching bag, and I am done with your abuse."

The color drained from Arra's face. The sweat dripped. Fortuna's voice was strong. Cold. Scary.

"So, here's the deal, Arrabiato, you keep your repulsive hands off my body, and I will leave your boys alone. Get out of line, even in the slightest, and I will find your boys and bring them to heel a little more each time. If you get my meaning.

"I'm done with your abuse, Arrabiato. DONE. Do you understand?"

Arrabiato was frozen in place. He was angry. He didn't like a woman threatening him. But Fortuna's voice sounded cold. Hard. He knew she meant every word. And he thought of the prospect of Fortuna's grip in the night.

His stomach churned. He went cold, her voice hissing in his ears.

The Murderous Lawlessness in a Nutshell

The end is here. I remain aghast and outraged at man's continued arrogance over the days and weeks since Roe v. Wade was revoked. The powerful men persist in their dismissive, lawless, and brutal denial, "Constitution? What Constitution?"

In the narrative of *The Heinous Murders of Countless 21st Century Women,* I have told the story of how volumes of documents and testimony that were harmful to the respective Supreme Court nominees were withheld, suppressed, and investigated in the least effective manner possible.

I have questioned the authority of the Supreme Court to unilaterally overturn Roe v. Wade. My research shows that there are two ways to change constitutional law, and neither of those ways gives the Court the right to do what the Court did in 2022.

I have called out the contradictions to constitutional law in the majority decision, written by Justice Samuel Alito, to justify the revocation of Roe v. Wade.

In short, I believe that we, as a nation, have wrongly trusted the word of the Supreme Court. We were primed to believe that the Court, under direction of the 45th president, was destined to overturn Roe v. Wade. We trusted, but failed to verify, the Supreme

Court's jurisdiction to revoke constitutional law.

In this, the final chapter of The Heinous Murders of Countless 21st Century Women, I shall make clear that the substance of the abortion laws are not the problem. The abortion laws are but the foul pus seeping from the infection of lawlessness. At the heart of the problem is man's penchant for thinking that he is above the law.

Throughout my narrative in *The Heinous Murders*, I have done my best to politely bring to light the lawmakers effective use of their "ignorance" of constitutional law to subjugate, to kill, and to threaten women for their selfish purposes. Texas is the Poster State for abortion ignorance and lawlessness. In the mid 1800s, Texas legislators decided women must be controlled so that only the right kind of babies are born. At that time, women were considered breeding stock to preserve the white patriarchy. Apparently, that vile viewpoint perseveres. White men fear the loss of their patriarchal power to the burgeoning nonwhite populations.

And throughout the months of research and writing of *The Heinous Murders*, I have watched and waited in despair for someone to call out the Red Cult states for willfully violating the Constitution. Lawmakers are intent upon protecting a mass of cells in a woman's womb, but have no regard for the woman in whose body the womb exists.

Yes, my words have been snarky in some places, and I shall continue to be snarky. For me, being snarky reduces the need to repeatedly shout, "Are you freaking kidding me?!"

The more I researched, the more I felt like I was in a surreal display of three-year-old children, all with serious cognitive and neurological impairments, running our country. For the most part, I have been relatively restrained in my narrative. However, this is my last opportunity to shout, in very unladylike fashion:

We women are being bamboozled by the Red Cult lawmakers! We have been judicially screwed by the Supreme Court of the United States. We are being run to ground by a posse of lawless lawmen who want to protect a "potential life," not our existing lives! These maniacal wretches are killing us in the name of laws that they are breaking to control us! No adult with authority is defending us!

I cannot be the only person who questions the Supreme Court's independent authority to revoke Roe v. Wade. Not only do I believe their action was wrong, but I also believe the Court used its considerable power unconstitutionally to achieve its ends. In doing so, the Court has subjected the nation's women to heinous torture in order to protect the nonexistent "states' rights."

We have trusted that the Court acted within the law and in allegiance to their oaths of office. We were wrong.

Since the beginning of their time on earth, men have selectively translated Scripture to subjugate women with their persistent-but-false Biblical-control charade. In like manner, man also has selectively interpreted Section 1 of the Fourteenth Amendment. They control women with pronouncements that we are not entitled to the protections under that amendment.

In devising their phony and illegitimate abortion laws, the states quickly cut to the end phrases of the Fourteenth Amendment that pertain to our right to life and liberty. In their artful use of the amendment, the state lawmakers slip by the first part, which says that states have *no right* to make laws that restrict rights.

Several times throughout my story (probably to your irritation), I have referenced three constitutional documents that are critical to our wellbeing—the Supremacy Clause of the Constitution, the Ninth Amendment, and the Fourteenth amendments in the Bill of Rights.. The Red Cult lawmakers have astutely ignored the first, totally avoided any reference to the significant information in the second, and ignored the critical and binding wording in the third.

Please, I implore you. Read these critical documents with me now. Carefully. This old journalist fears for the futures of her female progeny and of yours. The barbarians among the Red Cult have molded their interpretations and their selective use of these documents to suit their need to control their breeding stock.

The first document is the Supremacy Clause of the U.S. Constitution.

> "This Constitution, and the Laws of the United States … shall be the supreme Law of the Land; and the Judges in every State shall be bound thereby, any Thing in the Constitution or Laws of any State to the Contrary notwithstanding."[61]

> (*Author's note*: The missing text pertains to treaties, pursuant to, authorities and other legal expressions. I cut to the words that mean something to us women.)

> In normal terms, the Supremacy Clause means that judges in every state must follow the Constitution, laws, and treaties of the federal government in matters that are directly or indirectly within the government's control. *Thus, a federal court may require a state to stop certain behavior it believes interferes with, or is in conflict with, federal law.*" (Emphasis: author's)

> Seems reasonable to believe that Alabama's Supreme Court's questionable, God-like decree on a frozen embryo being a child falls within this constitutional prohibition. Just saying.

The second document is the Ninth Amendment, one of the 10 original amendments, adopted in 1791. The original language of the amendment is this:

> *"The enumeration in the Constitution of certain rights shall not be construed to deny or disparage others retained by the people."*[62]

What this means to regular folk is this:

> "The Ninth Amendment provides that the enumeration of certain rights in the Constitution should not be construed to mean that the Constitution does not protect rights that are not enumerated [listed]. The Amendment was included in the Bill of Rights to address fears that expressly protecting certain rights might be misinterpreted implicitly to sanction the infringement of others."

To my simple way of looking at things, this amendment is the underpinning of the Fourteenth Amendment. It says that we have rights that may not be noted in the Constitution, but, even unnamed, they are remain our rights. The Fourteenth Amendment reinforces that premise and that of the Supremacy Clause: states have only the rights granted by the Constitution and may not restrict any rights.

The third is Section 1 of the Fourteenth Amendment of the Bill of Rights.

> *All persons born or naturalized* in the United States, and subject to the jurisdiction thereof, *are citizens* of the United States and *of the State wherein they reside. No State shall make or enforce any law which shall abridge the privileges or immunities of citizens* of the United States; nor shall any State deprive any person of life, liberty, or property, without due process of law; nor deny to any person within its jurisdiction the equal protection of the laws. (Emphasis: The author's)

It is important to note here that the word *shall* in the amendment represents a symbolic pair of handcuffs, which obligates *state law to follow federal law*. In this case, state lawmakers *shall* keep their laws off a woman's right to make her own health-care decisions. And every other personal decision. On contraception. On marriage. Whatever grips the justices in their orgasmic sense of power. (Emphasis: author's.)

You may be thinking that I am too confident in my viewpoints about these constitutional laws. I appreciate your concern. I am, after all, just a laywoman. We women have been trained to be suspicious of any woman who presumes to question any man's actions and motives. Be that as it may, let me say, in all humility as a horribly flawed woman, it is possible that I failed to notice that Section 1 of the Fourteenth Amendment had been rendered irrelevant.

Nevertheless, the Bill of Rights of the Constitution remains intact and readily available to read. If any part of the Bill of Rights had been deleted from the Constitution, you and I would have heard or read about the seismic event somewhere. So, I remain confident that, to the aggravation of the powerful men, the Fourteenth Amendment stands as law, without any qualifications as defined by a Supreme Court beholden to the Red Cult.

While we are on the topic of changing the U.S. Constitution, such as to modify the Fourteenth Amendment, making that change is an involved and lengthy process. To change the Constitution:

> Congress must call a convention for proposing amendments upon application of the legislatures of two-thirds of the states (i.e., 34 of 50 states). Amendments proposed by Congress or convention become valid only when ratified by the legislatures of, or conventions in, three-fourths of the states (i.e., 38 of 50 states).[63]

None of that has happened, so I am on solid ground.

Justice Samuel Alito did his best to eliminate the Fourteenth Amendment throughout the majority decision. The wording implies, bit by bit, discriminatory insult by discriminatory insult, that the states' rights exceed the Constitution. According to the Fourteenth Amendment, the states have no rights here.

I'll let Justice Samuel Alito's insults and violations of constitutional law speak for themselves. In his majority opinion for the revocation of Roe v. Wade, Alito wrote (I have emphasized Alito's words throughout this section for clarity.)

- *"For the first 185 years after the adoption of the Constitution, each State was permitted to address this issue in accordance with the views of its citizens."*

This is a true statement of fact. However, Justice Alito neglected to tell the whole truth. The male decision makers have allowed those states to act in contravention of the U.S. Constitution. Those states continue to be just as lawless now.

- *"It is time to heed the Constitution and return the issue of abortion to the people's elected representative ..."*

From my perspective, this was a statement falsely and deliberately entitled the control-hungry Red Cult legislatures to pursue their "conspiracy against rights." (More on this later.)

- Roe v. Wade was wrong because *"It imposed the same highly restrictive regime on the entire Nation, and it effectively struck down the abortion laws of every single state."*

Wrong again, Justice Alito. Roe v. Wade righted the wrong of the Texas law and held all states to their constitutional obligation of silence on abortion. Of course, the states objected. For centuries, they had practiced control of women's rights with impunity.

- *"And in this case, 26 States have expressly asked the Court to overrule Roe and Casey and allow the States to regulate or prohibit pre-viability abortions."*

The whining from the lawless states heightened the Court's resolve with still more impetus to destroy Roe v. Wade.

Question for the majority Red Cult Supremes: Do you recall taking this oath, the one specific to the Court?

"I, __________, do solemnly swear (or affirm) that I will administer justice without respect to persons, and do equal right to the poor and to the rich, and that I will faithfully and impartially discharge and perform all the duties incumbent upon me as __________ under the Constitution and laws of the United States. So help me God."[64]

Your blatant allegiance to the Red Cult Master, to your egos, and to the Red Cult states suggest that you may have forgotten those words.

Because the Court, in violation of the Constitution, declared that the states had jurisdiction over abortion rights, and no one questioned the correctness of that statement, every group fighting for women's rights is chasing a faux fox. In an honorable society, the high Court would be a trusted authority. It once enjoyed that reputation. Now, however, the majority is anything but a trusted or honorable

(*Author's note:* : Please read the Dobb's reference on the majority opinion. The Court's majority allegiance to ensuring that a state has any right to our bodies and our decisions about or bodies is reprehensible. The Court's palpable disdain for and women's rights as human beings overwhelms.)

From this woman's perspective, SCOTUS willingly freed the petulant state lawmakers to willfully breach the sacred law of the land and to, once again, legislate their deadly—and medically unsound—laws. We have wrongly trusted that the legislatures have had the right to enact those laws. Because we have trusted, but not questioned, that states were acting in good faith, we have allowed those trusted authorities to get away with murder, under the guise of legislative prerogative. However, the Constitution squelches that entitlement.

Essentially, the decision-makers have been using the assumptive close in completing their arguments against women's rights. The "Indeed Career Guide"[65] explains the assumptive close this way. "Assumptive closing is a technique that salespeople use to encourage prospective buyers to make a purchase. It involves assuming that the customer has already agreed to make a purchase before they've explicitly done so." The lawmakers sold the farm, and we were denied the option to buy it. More to the point, they continue to assume that we shall not question their authority to control women's bodies.

The rights are ours under the Constitution, but, inasmuch as the state legislatures are not using the Constitution, we currently are without foundation for dispute. This is especially true because no one is saying on our behalf, "Hey! Wait a minute! You guys have no authority to make these laws!"

Not to put too fine a point on this, in case you haven't noticed, the majority of lawmakers treating women as irresponsible children are men. I believe this oversight results from our aged-old history of acquiescing to the illusion that men know what they are doing and have "our best interests" at heart. The visible truth of man's current interest is his power and control should give women renewed vigor, if not revitalized resolve, to fight for our rights under the Constitution.

In the majority decision, Justice Alito clearly wrote that "… the Constitution makes no reference to abortion …" Therefore, by the authority of the Supremacy Clause, of the Ninth Amendment, and of the Fourteenth Amendment, the states can adopt no laws pertaining to abortion in their constitutions.

States can, however, protect abortion rights. *Democracy Docket* asserts that, "While state constitutions cannot conflict with the national document, states are able to outline or clarify rights that go further than those in the federal Constitution."[66] As of this writing, at least 30 states and commonwealths have expanded abortion rights and enshrined abortion protections in their constitutions. Some male-dominated legislatures, such as Florida's Red Cult, are trying to repeal those constitutional protections.

The most appalling statement in the majority decision is, "The Court acknowledges that States have a legitimate interest in protecting 'potential life.'" Justice Alito repeatedly relies upon the fallacious premise that the states had any "legitimate interest" in any part of a woman's decision.

By what manner of law or judicial thinking does an amorphous collection of cells in the process of gestation have "rights"? Even greater rights and legal protections than are granted to the human who gives life through the gift of her own life in gestation. God anointed woman as the giver of life for all of eternity. Man, acting as God, is now declaring that "potential life" has greater rights than God's anointed life. These men are delusional in their entitlement.

According to the Constitution, the amorphous process of gestation is not part of "We the people …" The states, supported by the Court, are conferring rights to a "promise" that are not theirs to confer without due process. That due process must include scientific facts about personhood to determine the legal status of that amorphous collection in relation to constitutional law. The states have shown no interest in scientific facts.

In the body of *The Heinous Murders*, I have raised three significant questions. Before I began writing, I posed them to my lawyer friends and, then, to the constitutional specialists. The first group supported my perspectives on those questions; the other group sent crickets.

What procedure or legal mechanism gives the Court the independent authority to revoke constitutional precedent? Who had standing to bring the case for revocation? In their zeal to satisfy their allegiance to the president, not to the law, were the justices guilty of conspiracy against rights, as the president himself was charged in his attempt to prohibit the rights of voters?

The "What"
The cases that come before the Court are initiated through a petition for a writ of certiorari. The writ is a request that the Supreme Court order a lower court to send up the record of the case for review. The Court receives about 7,000 writs of certiorari a year; it accepts between 100 and 150 of those petitions.

Once the Court decides to hear a case, the Court then uses Judicial Review (established in 1803) to evaluate these cases between entities at odds over laws. The Court weighs the legal arguments, as they pertain to questions of law, presented by attorneys for litigants X v. Y.

The complex role of the Supreme Court in this system derives from its authority to invalidate legislation or executive actions which, in the Court's considered judgment, conflict with the Constitution.

The "Who"

Who had standing in overturning Roe v. Wade? No one. This was not a case brought before the Court for judicial review and disposition. Interestingly, Roe's fate coincided with the Court's revival of the writ for Dobbs v. Jackson Women's Health Organization in Mississippi. The case, which challenged the state's 15-week abortion, had been held in abeyance since 2020.

It took some care to find the actual Dobbs case because my searches repeatedly turned up the same documents justifying the revocation of Roe and Casey (the case that backed up Roe). Finally, my research showed that the Court had used the Dobbs case to open an illicit backdoor to revoke Roe and Casey, surreptitiously.

As a matter of interest, Justice Ruth Bader Ginsberg, a pro-law and pro-abortion jurist, was still sitting on the Court when it accepted the Dobbs petition. The Court scheduled and relisted *Dobbs* for more than eight months.[67]

Being quite cynical, I suspect the Red Cult Supremes were waiting for Ginsberg to make her involuntary exit from her seat and for President Trump to appoint the deciding vote in overturning Roe. I did not spend time running down the intrigue behind that distasteful premise.

Once the final Roe foe was installed on the Court, the majority exercised its hubris and slipped the overturning of Roe under the cover of upholding the Mississippi law banning abortions after 15 weeks. Again, no writ of certiorari had been submitted to review the overturning of Roe v. Wade.

No writ was available because no lower court had heard and judged any case involving Roe v. Wade. Without a writ, the Court had no case for judicial review. More than 80% of the country wanted Roe to stand, so no one had initiated action in any lower court.

So, the Court upheld Dobbs. Then, behind the scenes, the Court used the cover of Dobbs to unilaterally revoke the 50 years of precedent. Alito justified the surreptitious act by saying, "Twenty-six states had asked the Court to do so." No writ of certiorari accompanied the bogus request.

The law that gave women equal protection under law ended in a whimper, covertly. No oral arguments. No nothing. The majority threw women to the rapacious packs of wolves in the Red Cult states. The unconstitutional laws enacted by those states have jeopardized or ended the lives of thousands of women across the nation.

The "Conspiracy Against Rights"

In Chapter 4, I said that I believed the majority justices may be guilty of "conspiracy against rights." The law, 18 U.S.C. § 242, makes it a crime for someone acting under color of law, which the members of the majority did, to willfully deprive a person of a right or privilege protected by the Constitution or laws of the United States.[68]

Although Neil Gorsuch, Brett Kavanaugh, and Amy Coney Barrett, the three Trump appointees, may not have exactly lied under oath, they did give the Senate Judiciary Committee the firm idea that Roe v. Wade was safe with them. Then, with the benefit of a majority of Roe foes, Alito salved his ego, and Trump was triumphant in achieving his campaign promise. The fix was satisfactorily consummated. (Chapter 3 details the testimonies of the appointees.)

As I think a bit more about the "conspiracy against rights" law, I believe the fanatical state legislators may also fall into the "conspiracy against rights" box. Legislators in each of the Red Cult states conspired with each other to prevent women from enjoying their constitutional rights.

Perhaps you think I have provided too many details. I think not. The lawmakers maintain their assumptive close, which still is accepted without question. We trusting folk continue to believe because the authorities have persuaded us to believe that states have the right to abridge a woman's right to life and liberty.

A woman's future freedom from oppression and being treated as breeding stock depends upon her knowing how deceitfully she is being disrespected and abused in the name of the white patriarchy. Every woman needs to know, firsthand where her rights stand, how strongly they stand, and how disdainfully the lawmakers regard women.

The question now is, so what? The "so what" is this. Only we women can change this outrage. The male-dominated bodies of lawmakers have no interest in abiding by the laws set out in the Constitution. Protecting the patriarchy is their goal.

Powerful men have reduced our worth to our ability to breed the right kind and color of baby to preserve the patriarchy.

Powerful women can establish the equality that God intended when he created "them [man and woman] in our [God as man and woman] image." Genesis 2:7. God expected a balanced team of humans to create His world. Men installed themselves as our overseers. Have we noticed yet how well their world authority is working out?

Women and the men who love and revere them can restore His plan, His will.

Most importantly, men are misdirecting our attention away from their lawlessness. They keep women busy chasing the symptom of the loss of Roe v. Wade while they continue to spew the pus of their disdain for and their lordliness over their breed stock.

If being called "breeding stock" offends you, then it's time to rise up with the fierce determination to call out the liars and the abusers on the Supreme Court and in the Red Cult legislatures.

My Outrage in Summary

"What about the murders." You ask.

That's a very good question. A fair one.

However, it is one I cannot answer. A series of events over the two years since the Supreme Court of the United States exceeded its authority and overturned Roe v. Wade, have us engaged in a muddle of anger and hysteria and righteous indignation.

First, Justice Samuel Alito, erroneously defending states' rights in his majority opinion, rather than upholding the rights on individuals, gave states the unconstitutional authority to determine abortion rights. Giddy with authority from SCOTUS, the male-dominated legislatures enacted numerous heinous abortion laws. The laws affected a woman's right to make her own reproductive-health decisions in concert with her physician.

The most heinous aspect of their didactic decisions lay in the fact that those men, as a group, acted without benefit of the requisite medical license. They presumed an authority over a woman's life that exceeded their legislative boundaries and willfully endangered the lives of pregnant women.

The male-dominated legislators and the male-dominated courts have divorced themselves from all responsibility associated with the baby-making process. Women are solely responsible for their pregnancies. Despite the scientific fact that not a single baby begins to grow in the womb without a sperm attaching itself to an egg, the men blame the woman for "getting pregnant."

Women die in childbirth. This is a well-documented fact. The Morbidity and Mortality Weekly Report keeps extensive records on deaths in childbirth, which are on the rise in states that have the most rigid and heinous abortion laws.

We can't officially call the deaths as a result of abortion restrictions "murders." We have allowed the Supreme Court to escape its responsibility for its illicit revocation of Roe v. Wade. So, we are forced to adhere to an illicit decision.

Neither can we officially call death in childbirth a murder, even when the death results from the heinous laws that interfere with a woman's right to determine her own reproductive care. Laws imposed by legislatures acting as medical personnel without a medical license still are not considered murderous. Personally, I consider such outrageous impertinence a murderous imposition upon a women's well-being and her right to life, liberty, and due process under our Constitution.

These lawmakers lay our deaths-by-baby at our feet. We aren't being murdered by ignorant, arrogant men. We are committing suicide by flouting their authoritarian abortion laws. Our deaths have nothing to do with their depraved indifference to women's rights as human beings.

The lawmakers are intent upon protecting the product of their seed, the fetal life, rather than the life that is the fount of all human life. In Chapter 7, I have documented their perverse pursuit of protecting the white patriarchy.

What outrages me more than anything is the failure of the esteemed news media to ask the important questions that could have/would have changed the direction of this deadly game of baby roulette.

The journalists, all of them, jumped on the hysteria bandwagon. "The sky is falling! The sky is falling!" I don't mean to make light of the very real crisis of losing such critical constitutional rights. But from my perspective as a retired journalist, journalists cannot, must not stop at "The sky is falling!"

Based upon my research, not a one asked herself if the Supreme Court had the authority to unilaterally revoke a 50-year precedent. The answer is: it did not.

We believed that SCOTUS was bound to revoke Roe, so we believed it was a done deal. We also assumed that the Court would act honorably and in accord with established rules and procedures. We trusted but failed to verify. We failed critical thinking on the critical topic.

Not a single journalist raised questions about the statements in Alito's majority opinion. As I have reported, he declared that it was "time to return the subject of abortion to the states." He, a respected Supreme Court Justice, flouted constitutional law and gave the states the authority to impose the heinous laws that violated individual rights. He granted states the unconstitutional right to kill, maim, and terrorize women.

The answer to the question unasked by journalists is: according to the Fourteenth Amendment of the United States Constitution, states are *prohibited* from enacting any law that exceeds the federal constitution. Alito declared that by the Court's action the U.S. Constitution was free of reference to abortion. So, the states were prohibited from imposing *any* abortion bans.

Not to put too fine a point on this, I seriously wondered whether any of the journalists, whom I have revered for decades, had read even the summary of the Dobbs decision or the amendments in the Bill of Rights as they pertained to Roe v. Wade and the revocation of that critical law.

I am a feisty, unsophisticated, retired journalist who writes nonfiction narratives, such as this one. If I, with my seriously restricted resources, have been able to learn how blatantly the Court and the states have bamboozled us to control us, then the respected news organizations with their great resources should have been able to write the truth. The truth about the Court exceeding its authority, Alito's self-serving and egregiously wrong majority opinion, and the states' violation of constitutional law.

Someone with clout needs to step out in order to save women from the terror they have experienced. The journalists fell into the narrative the Red Cult wanted to promote and failed to pursue the truth with the megaphone of their august reputations.

Mine is a small voice shouting against the hurricane of misinformation in "the sky is falling" drama. If the journalists could join their voices, they might well save lives and return our country to constitutional law that benefits all of us—including women.

And for the record, my research shows that the Court needs writs of certiorari to revoke the laws that protect contraception/birth control, marriage of any kind, and whatever other laws justices Alito and Clarence Thomas believe they can revoke on their own.

References

1. Anderson, Meg. *Who is Christine Blasey Ford, the Woman Accusing Brett Kavanaugh.* NPR. https://www.npr.org/2018/09/17/648803684/ who-is-christine- blasey-ford-the-woman-accusing-brett-kavanaugh-of-sexual-assault. Sept. 17, 2020

2. Oliva, Jennifer, Prof. *More than 800 women law profs demand Senate reject Kavanaugh.* People's World. https://www.peoplesworld.org/article/more-than-800-women-law-profs-demand-senate-reject-kavanaugh/ October 4, 2018.

3. Svrluga, Susan. *'Unfathomable': More than 2,400 law professors sign letter opposing Kavanaugh's confirmation.* The Washington Post. https://www.washingtonpost.com/education/2018/10/04/ unprecedented- unfathomable-more-than-law-professors-sign-letter-after-kavanaugh-hearing/ October 4, 2018.

4. Engle, Kathleen. Prof. Suffolk University Law School. *More than 800 women law profs demand Senate reject Kavanaugh.* People's World. https://www.peoplesworld.org/article/more-than-800-women-law-profs-demand-senate-reject-kavanaugh/ October 4, 2018.

5. McKanders, Karla. *More than 800 women law profs demand Senate reject Kavanaugh*. People's World. https://www.peoplesworld.org/article/more-than-800-women-law-profs-demand-senate-reject-kavanaugh/ October 4, 2018.

6. Gore, D'Angelo, Farley, Robert, Robertson, Lori. *What Gorsuch, Kavanaugh and Barrett Said About Roe at Confirmation Hearings.*https://www.factcheck.org/2022/05/what-gorsuch-kavanaugh-and-barrett-said-about-roe-at-confirmation-hearings/ June 24, 2022.

7. Hughes, Chief Justice Charles E. *The republic endures and this is the symbol of faith.* Supreme Court of the United States. https://www.supremecourt.gov/about/constitutional.pdf October 13, 1932.

8. Alito, Justice Samuel (Majority). *Dobbs v. Jackson Women's Health Organization 2022.* Supreme Court Case. National Constitution Center. pp 1 https://constitution-center.org/the-constitution/supreme-court-case-library/dobbs-v-jackson-womens-health-organization

9. Ibid.

10. *Uncovering the Truth About Supreme Court Justice Kavanaugh* https://www.americanoversight.org/investigation/uncovering-the-truth-about-supreme-court-nominee-kavanaughstice. American Oversight. July 27, 2020.

11. Ibid.

12. Ibid.

13. Kavanaugh, Judge Brett. Christine Blasey Ford. https://www.judiciary.senate.gov/imo/media/doc/09.17.18%20BMK%20Interview%20Transcript%20(Redacted).pdf Sept. 17, 2018.

14. Kavanaugh, Judge Brett. Deborah Ramirez preview. Senate Judiciary Committee. Washington, DC. https://www.judiciary.senate.gov/imo/media/doc/09.25.18%20BMK%20Interview%20Transcript%20(Redacted).pdf Sept. 25, 2018

15. Kavanaugh, Judge Brett. Julia Swetnick preview. Senate Judiciary Committee. Washington, DC. https://www.judiciary.senate.gov/imo/media/doc/09.26.18%20BMK%20Interview%20Transcript%20(Redacted).pdf Sept. 26, 2018

16. Totenberg, Nina. *Transcript of NPR Report on Anita Hill's charges of sexual harassment by Clarence Thomas.* Weekend Edition. https://jwa.org/media/transcript-of-nina-totenbergs-npr-report-on-anita-hills-charges-of-sexual-harassment-by-0 Oct. 6, 1991

17. Ibid

18. Ibid.

19. Ibid.

20. *Reservation on Judge Amy Coney Barrett's Qualification for Supreme Court.* New York Bar Association. https://www.nycbar.org/blogs/reservations-on-judge-amy-coney-barretts-qualifications-for-supreme-court/ Oct. 23, 2020.

21. *About the Supreme Court.* United States Courts. https://www.uscourts.gov/about-federal-courts/educational-resources/about-educational-outreach/activity-resources/about

22. Patrick, John. *Judicial Review* Annenberg Classroom. https://www.annenbergclassroom.org/glossary_term/judicial-review/

23. Hughes, Chief Justice Charles E. *The republic endures and this is the symbol of faith.* Supreme Court of the United States. https://www.supremecourt.gov/about/constitutional.pdf October 13, 1932.

24. Wex Definitions Team. *Dobbs v. Jackson Women's Health Organization* (2022). Legal Information Institute. Cornell Law School. https://www.law.cornell.edu/wex/dobbs_v._jackson_women%27s_health_organization_%282022%29 June 2022.

25. Indeed Editorial Team. *The Assumptive Close Technique.* Indeed Career Guide. https://www.indeed.com/career-advice/career-development/assumptive-closing

26. FindLaw Staff. *Article III Standing Requirements.* FindLaw. https://constitution.findlaw.com/article3/annotation10.html June 27, 2022.

27. Sullivan, Caroline. *The Power of State Constitutions.* Democracy Docket. https://www.democracydocket.com/analysis/the-power-of-state-constitutions/ July 26, 2022.

28. Barnett, Randy E. and Seidman, Louis Michael. *The Ninth Amendment Common Interpretation.* National Constitution Center. https://constitutioncenter.org/the-constitution/amendments/amendment-ix/interpretations/131

29. Title 18, U.S.C., Section 241 - Conspiracy Against Rights. Federal Civil Rights Statutes. What We Investigate—FBI. https://www.fbi.gov/investigate/civil-rights/federal-civil-rights-statutes. Jan 17, 2023

30. Cole, Devan. *Alito told Ted Kennedy that he respected Roe v. Wade, according to excerpts from late senator's diary in* The New York Times.

31. Gore, D'Angelo, Farley, Robert, Robertson, Lori. *What Gorsuch, Kavanaugh and Barrett Said About Roe at Confirmation Hearings.* https://www.factcheck.org/2022/05/what-gorsuch-kavanaugh-and-barrett-said-about-roe-at-confirmation-hearings/ June 24, 2022.

32. Ibid.

33. Ibid

34. Ibid.

35. Alito, Justice Samuel (Majority). *Dobbs v. Jackson Women's Health Organization 2022.* Supreme Court Case. National Constitution Center. https://constitutioncenter.org/the-constitution/supreme-court-case- library/Dobbs-v-jackson-womens-health-organization

36. Article VI, Clause 2. Supremacy Clause. Constitution Annotated. https://constitution.congress.gov/browse/essay/artVI-C2-1/ALDE_00013395/

37. *Historical Abortion Timeline: 1850 to Today.* Planned Parenthood. https://www.plannedparenthoodaction.org/issues/abortion/abortion-central-history-reproductive-health-care-america/historical-abortion-law-timeline-1850-today

38. Ibid.

39. Alito, Justice Samuel (Majority). *Dobbs v. Jackson Women's Health Organization 2022.* Supreme Court Case. National Constitution Center. https://constitutioncenter.org/the-constitution/supreme-court-case- library/dobbs-v-jackson-womens-health-organization

40. Chutkan, Judge Tanya. United States of America v. Donald J. Trump. Criminal action No. 23-257 (TSC *455(a)*. United States District Court. District of Columbia. Dec. 12, 2023.

41. The Federalist Society. Washington, DC. 2024. https://fedsoc.org/about-us

42. Hughes, Chief Justice Charles E. *The republic endures and this is the symbol of faith*. Supreme Court of the United States. https://www.supremecourt.gov/about/constitutional.pdf   October 13, 1932.

43. Kilanoff, Eleanor. *Not 1925: Texas' law banning abortion dates to before the Civil War.* https://www.texastribune.org/2022/08/17/texas-abortion-law-history/   Texas Tribune. Aug. 17, 2022.

44. Ibid.

45. Ibid.

46. Ibid.

47. Klibanoff, Eleanor; Borah, Neelam. *Judge says woman may abort fetus with lethal abnormality*. Texas Tribune. Dec. 7, 2023.

48. Smyth, Julie Carr. *Ohio Woman Who Miscarried at Home Won't be Charged with Corpse Abuse, Grand Jury Decides*. AP. Jan. 11,, 2024. https://apnews.com/article/miscarriage-prosecution-ohio-brittany-watts-68145b3044b3cc61017b71a97f7cc036

49. *Historical Abortion Timeline: 1850 to Today*. Planned Parenthood. https://www.plannedparenthoodaction.org/issues/abortion/abortion-central-history-reproductive-health-care-america/historical-abortion-law-timeline-1850-today

50. Poston, Dudley L, Jr.; Saénz, Rogelio. *The U.S. White Majority will soon disappear forever.* The Conversation. https://theconversation.com/the-us-white-majority-will-soon-disappear-forever-115894

51. Ibi Hoyert, Donna L., PhD. *Maternal Mortality Rates in the United States, 2021.* National Center for Health Statistics. 2021.NCHS Health E-Stats. 2023. https://www.cdc.gov/nchs/data/hestat/maternal-mortality/2021/maternal -mortality-rates-2021.htm

52. *The Bill or Rights: A Brief History.* ACLU. March 4, 2002. https://www.aclu.org/documents/bill-rights-brief-history

53. Chutkan, Judge Tanya. *Defendant Donald J. Trump's Motion for Recusal of District Judge Pursuant to 28 U.S.C. § 455(a).* United States District Court. District of Columbia. Dec. 12, 2023. https://www.democracydocket.com/wp-content/uploads/2023/08/50-2023- 09-11-mot-for-recusal.pdf

54. Blair, Gabrielle. *Ejaculate Responsibly; A Whole New Way To Think About Abortion.* New York. Workman Publishing. 2022.

55. Ibid.

56. Ibid.

57. Ibid.

58. Ibid.

59. Ibid.

60. Karimi, Faith. CNN. *South African doctor invents female condom with "teeth" to fight rape.* Inside Africa. http://www.cnn.com/2010/WORLD/africa/06/20/south.africa.female.condom/index.html. June 21, 2010.

61. Article VI, Clause 2. Supremacy Clause. Constitution Annotated. https://constitution.congress.gov/browse/essay/artVI-C2-1/ALDE_00013395/

62. Ninth Amendment. Annenberg Classroom. https://www.annenbergclassroom.org/ninth-amendment/

63. Constitutional Convention. Common Interpretation. National Constitution Center. https://constitutioncenter.org/the-constitution/articles/article-v/interpretations/277

64. *Oaths of Office*. About the Court. Supreme Court of the United States. https://www.supremecourt.gov/about/oath/oathsofoffice.aspx

65. Indeed Editorial Team. *The Assumptive Close Technique.* Indeed Career Guide. https://www.indeed.com/career-advice/career-development/assumptive-closing

66. Sullivan, Caroline. *The Power of State Constitutions.* Democracy Docket. https://www.democracydocket.com/analysis/the-power-of-state-constitutions/ July 26, 2022.

67. Gore, D'Angelo, Farley, Robert, Robertson, Lori. *What Gorsuch, Kavanaugh and Barrett Said About Roe at Confirmation Hearings.* https://www.factcheck.org/2022/05/what-gorsuch-kavanaugh-and-barrett-said-about-roe-at-confirmation-hearings/ June 24, 2022.

68. Title 18, U.S.C., Section 241 - Conspiracy Against Rights. Federal Civil Rights Statutes. What We Investigate—FBI. https://www.fbi.gov/investigate/civil-rights/federal-civil-rights-statutes. Jan 17, 2023

www.ingramcontent.com/pod-product-compliance
Lightning Source LLC
Chambersburg PA
CBHW020325180726
47991CB00019B/695